TOP **10**
BOSTON

CONTENTS

BOSTON

INTRODUCING

Downtown Boston cityscape

WELCOME TO
BOSTON

Quaint brownstones and polished skyscrapers; revolutionary relics and innovative universities. This scenic city celebrates its storied past while looking steadfastly to the future. Don't want to miss a thing? With Top 10 Boston, you'll enjoy the very best the city has to offer.

Boston is nicknamed "The Hub of the Universe" for good reason – simply put, it has it all (and then some). It brims with history (no surprise, given it was founded in 1630), with the Freedom Trail telling the story of the early days of colonial Boston and its role in the American Revolution.

Charlestown Navy Yard is one of the nation's oldest shipbuilding facilities, and was a center of technical innovation in the 19th century; today, this baton is taken up by the city's world-renowned universities and technological hubs, like Harvard University and MIT. Beyond the downtown

Old meets new in lively Boston

core of centuries-old buildings and revolutionary-era stomping grounds, Boston is known for its arts and creativity; there's no missing the Museum of Fine Arts, which houses the largest Asian art collection in the country, or the Isabella Stewart Gardner Museum, with masterpieces by the likes of Botticelli on display.

Beyond its rich history and cultural clout, Boston is a dream for those who want to eat, shop, or simply stroll. You could spend your morning browsing local fashion boutiques, get lost amid paperbacks in cozy bookshops in the afternoon, and end the day watching the Boston Red Sox on the small screen at a no-frills dive bar. There's plenty of space to embrace the outdoors, too, whether you toss a football about on Boston Common or take a stroll along the Boston Harborwalk. All of this activity is best fueled by the city's fabulous food scene. New England favorites like lobster boil and clam chowder are served up ocean-side in the Waterfront district, while lip-smacking pizza, pasta, and cannoli attract the crowds in the North End, home to Boston's long-standing Italian American community.

So, where to start? With Top 10 Boston, of course. This pocket-sized guide gets to the heart of the city with simple lists of 10, expert local knowledge, and comprehensive maps, helping you turn an ordinary trip into an extraordinary one.

THE STORY OF
BOSTON

Boston has continually transformed over the centuries. It's been a Puritan settlement, a crucible of the American Revolution, and a hub for immigrants seeking a better life. And today? It's a progressive center of creativity. Here's the story of how it came to be.

Early Settlers

For thousands of years, the region around Boston has hosted a tapestry of Indigenous cultures – two prominent groups being the Massachusett and the Wampanoag. The rocky Shawmut Peninsula, on which modern-day Boston sits, was used by both communities as a fishing and shellfish-gathering site. The arrival of Europeans in the 17th century proved disastrous for the Indigenous peoples, as the introduction of new diseases decimated the population.

The first European to permanently live in the area was William Blackstone (or Blaxton), who settled here in 1625. In 1630, he encouraged several hundred Puritans from the nearby Charlestown Colony to move to the area, which had a better water supply thanks to its natural springs. The settlement was later named Boston by one of its leaders, Isaac Johnson, after his hometown in Lincolnshire, England. It became the centerpiece of the Massachusetts Bay Colony, chartered by English king, Charles I.

Expansion and Decline

As the main trading hub of the Massachusetts Bay Colony, Boston blossomed into a lucrative port city for the British Empire. Timber and salt fish were two of the main exports, while imports included molasses from the Caribbean, which led to a wealth of rum distilleries popping up in the city.

An illustration depicting the 1630s Massachusetts Bay Colony

General Washington in Boston after the siege of the city ended in 1776

Although Boston was not as active in the transatlantic slave trade as the likes of Charleston in South Carolina, many wealthy Bostonians still profited via their investments in sugar plantations.

By the mid-1700s, however, Boston's prominence as a port had begun to decline. This was in part due to the rise of cities farther south, such as Philadelphia, that geographically sit closer to markets in the South and in the Caribbean.

A Revolutionary Role

In the 1760s, the imposition of British trade restrictions and taxation led to strained relations between the British and both Boston and the rest of the American colonies. It wasn't until 1773, however, that things reached breaking point following the Tea Act. Enraged by this British law, which was perceived as yet another attempt at taxation without representation, a small faction of Bostonians boarded an English ship and tossed its tea shipment into Boston Harbor. Following this, the British closed the harbor and declared martial law.

Rebellion eventually ignited into revolution in April 1775, with the first skirmishes of the Revolutionary War taking place near Boston in Lexington and Concord. At the same time, the city was involved in its own battle, the Siege of Boston, which saw General George Washington fight against British forces for almost a year, before the latter withdrew on March 17, 1776.

Moments in History

1636
Harvard, the colonies' first college, is founded by the Great and General Court of the Massachusetts Bay Colony.

1691
English monarchs William III and Mary II combine the Massachusetts Bay Colony with the Plymouth Colony to the south.

1713
The Old State House becomes the seat of British government in Boston.

1760
A massive fire tears through Boston, ultimately leaving hundreds of buildings destroyed and over a thousand residents without homes.

1775
The Battle of Bunker Hill takes place, one of the first major engagements of the Revolution.

1831

The New England Anti-Slavery Society is founded by William Lloyd Garrison, the editor of *The Liberator*.

1897

The first Boston Marathon is held, with just ten runners completing the race. Trophies were given to the first two.

1912

Fenway Park, the oldest major league ballpark and home of the Boston Red Sox, opens. It remains America's most iconic baseball park.

1958

The Freedom Trail is established, connecting sights associated with the American Revolution on a clearly marked route.

2019

Roxbury's Nubian Square receives its current name – a testament to the neighborhood's deep ties to African American culture.

Immigration and Expansion

Following the end of the Revolution in 1783, Boston's maritime trade swung back into action. As the ports of the British Empire were closed to US ships, those surging out of Boston Harbor set sail for the likes of France, Spain, and China. These new trade routes attracted immigrants to Boston, as did the opportunity to work on the railroads and canals that were swiftly spreading across the New England region, financed by Boston investors. The first major influx came from those attempting to escape Ireland's Great Famine in the mid-19th century; they were followed later by those from China and Italy. To house this growing population, the city undertook ambitious land reclamation efforts, creating districts like South End, Back Bay, and Chinatown. Some of the towns surrounding Boston – including Roxbury, Brighton, and Dorchester – were also brought under the control of the city.

At the same time as Boston grew in both size and population, the city emerged as a proponent for social change in the region. It was a major advocate for abolition during the

1800s, including serving as a stop along the Underground Railroad, and also fostered a thriving women's suffrage movement. This period also saw the city's cultural scene blossom. The now-renowned Museum of Fine Arts was set up in 1870, with the Boston Symphony Orchestra following in 1881; in addition, many publishers arrived and prestigious centers of learning, such as MIT and Boston University, were founded.

Boston Builds Skyward

The early 20th century saw the city's cultural offerings expand even further, with the Boston Opera House and Isabella Stewart Gardner Museum established. Spectator sports also thrived, thanks partly to the success of the Red Sox, who won baseball's World Series four times before 1918, and the Boston Bruins, who made their debut into ice hockey in 1924. The 1930s, meanwhile, saw the birth of Boston's jazz scene, thanks to the 40,000 African Americans who moved here to work in the city's Naval Shipyard.

The latter half of the 20th century, however, saw some tensions grow in

Michelle Wu speaking outside City Hall during her mayoral campaign

the city. During the 1950s, the urban development of the West End saw thousands of working-class Jewish and Italian immigrants displaced, and the docklands area – which had been cut off by an elevated freeway – deteriorate. Further issues arose in the 1970s, when the desegregation of public schools in the city led to riots and racial protests.

Boston Today

In the 21st century, thanks partly to its world-class universities such as Harvard and MIT, Boston has cemented itself as a leader in business, biotechnology, and artificial intelligence, and it's no surprise that several thousand startups operate across the city. Alongside a boom in forward-thinking businesses, Boston's population has also continued to grow; as well as a large Black community, there is also a growing number of Asian and Hispanic residents, who are adding their own heritage to this majority minority city. Beyond this, Boston is often regarded as one of the most progressive cities in the US. In November 2003, the Massachusetts Supreme Court in Boston legalized same-sex marriage – the first US state to do so – while 2021 saw the election of Michelle Wu as city mayor, the first woman and person of color to be elected to the office.

Crowds gathering in Boston to campaign for women's rights

TOP 10
EXPERIENCES

Planning the perfect trip to Boston? Whether you're visiting for the first time or making a return trip, there are some things you simply shouldn't miss out on. To make the most of your time – and to enjoy the very best this wonderfully varied city has to offer – be sure to add these experiences to your list.

1 Walk in the footsteps of history

In a city where historic sights and reminders of nation-shaping stories can be found around every corner, walking both the Freedom Trail *(p22)* and the Black Heritage Trail *(p86)* are a must. You'll get to know Boston's role in the American Revolution and Abolitionism.

2 Game day

Join thousands of passionate fans and secure tickets to see the legendary Boston Red Sox play a game at the most revered field in baseball, Fenway Park *(p119)*. You'll be so close to the action you'll hear the sharpe crack of the bat and the pop of the pitch in the catcher's mitt.

3 Tuck into spectacular seafood

Fish fans will love the city's signature clam chowder or a humble Boston "scrod" – the catch of the day, broiled with butter, lemon, and white wine. But, of course, lobster tops Boston's seafood offering; enjoy it at its best at the Barking Crab *(p103)*.

4 Bike the Emerald Necklace

A chain of parks forms the city's Emerald Necklace *(p29)*, making it perfect for a day out on two wheels. From the blooming flowerbeds of the Public Garden, pedal along the streamside bowers of Muddy River to the Arnold Arboretum.

5 Browse bookstores
Boston is home to countless bookstores. Head to Harvard Square (*p72*) to browse the shelves of the stores or try Trident Booksellers & Café (*p95*) on Newbury Street. Then grab a coffee and get lost in the pages of your purchase.

6 Listen to live music
Symphonic orchestras, jazz and blues, folk music, and alternative rock: Boston's sonorous music has something for every ear (*p62*). Venues can get booked up really quickly, so remember to buy tickets for events ahead.

7 Take a photo of quintessential Boston
Context is key when photographing Boston cityscapes. Step back from the Old State House (*p105*) to capture it surrounded by a forest of skyscrapers, a visual representation of the city's mix of old and new architecture.

8 Be inspired by cutting-edge art
The city's rich and extensive collection of contemporary art is at once challenging and captivating. To see major shows dedicated to current luminaries, visit the Institute of Contemporary Art (*p100*).

9 Visit the city's top museums
Boston's biggest export is knowledge. Science, sport, subcultures – whatever you want to learn about, there's a museum for it. A visit to one of the museums at Harvard University (*p30*) is a great place to start.

10 Escape to the beach
Hop on a ferry (May–Oct) from Long Wharf to Boston Harbor Islands (*p54*) and picnic on a beach with a book in hand. Or, head south of the city where miles of beaches (*p80*) await on Cape Cod, Martha's Vineyard, and Nantucket.

ITINERARIES

Treading the paths of history, enjoying superb seafood, or cheering on the Red Sox: there's a lot to see and do in Boston. With places to eat, drink, or simply take in the view, these itineraries offer ways to spend 2 days and 4 days in the city.

2 DAYS

Day 1

Morning
Start the day with a trip to Acorn Street, a treasured Beacon Hill (p84) photo spot that's rife with rustic cobblestones and picturesque row houses. Next, make your way to two idyllic green spaces – Boston Common and Public Garden (p28). First stroll through the Public

> **EAT**
> If you're in need of a quick bite on the go as you explore the North End, Bova's Bakery (p102) has been a local favorite since 1932 thanks to its cannolis, specialty cookies, bread, cakes, and other Italian favorites.

Acorn Street in the historic district of Beacon Hill

Garden, marveling at polished statues and watching the swan boats along the way, before entering neighboring Boston Common. Established in 1634, this site serves as the oldest city park in the nation, with towering monuments, curious squirrels darting about, and the Frog Pond. By now you've probably worked up an appetite. Head to nearby JM Curley (p108), where there's no shortage of burgers up for grabs.

Afternoon
After a hearty lunch, it's time to hit the Freedom Trail (p22). Begin at the Granary Burying Ground (p105) to pay your respects to iconic American luminaries, then continue northeast to visit sites like King's Chapel (p106) and the 1710s-era Old State House (p105) before arriving at Faneuil Hall (p105), formerly a popular place for impassioned political speeches. Pop into neighboring Quincy Market, which is filled with food stalls and shops. Once you've snagged the perfect souvenir, head up Mercantile Street to North End to visit Paul Revere House (p99) and Copps Hill Burying Ground (p99). End the day with a feast at Regina Pizzeria (p103), a cozy spot that's earned nationwide acclaim for its top-tier pies.

Day 2

Morning
Today kicks off with a stroll through Chinatown (p110), a bustling district that is adorned with a traditional

Chinese gateway. Fuel up on caffeine with a Vietnamese iced coffee at Pho Pasteur (p116), then head for some retail therapy at Essex Corner (p114) to peruse trinkets. To continue your shopping spree, walk along Boylston Street to reach Back Bay (p90). Here, you'll encounter boutique stores along Newbury Street (p34), but be sure to also make a quick pit stop to admire the ornate Trinity Church (p40). Once you're ready for lunch, seek out the Banks Fish House (p97) for a lobster roll paired with a bowl of New England clam chowder.

Wandering along elegant Newbury Street, home to upscale shops

Afternoon

Make your way to Back Bay Station and hop on the "T" to Andrew Station to

> **VIEW**
> Searching for a truly remarkable perspective on the city? Head up to Back Bay's View Boston (viewboston.com) to find 360-degree views from the 52nd floor of Prudential Tower.

explore South Boston (p132), where two sites in particular are worth visiting. The first is Carson Beach (p61), which serves as a top spot for swimming and beach volleyball, and the second is Dorchester Heights (p53), where you'll discover the crucial role that this landmark played during the War for Independence. After all this activity, reward yourself with a trip north to the iconic L Street Tavern (p136) – a rustic bar that featured in the film Good Will Hunting – before hopping back on the "T" to return to the heart of Boston, for a lavish dinner at O Ya (p109).

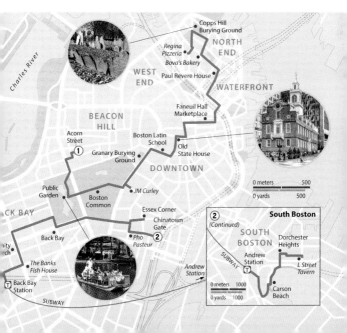

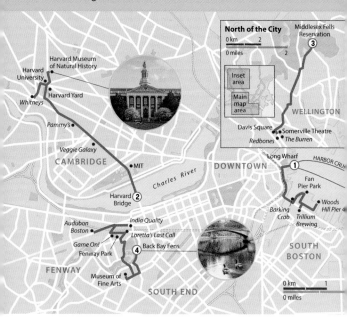

North of the City

0 km   2
0 miles   2

Middlesex Fells Reservation ③

Inset area

Main map area

WELLINGTON

Harvard Museum of Natural History

Harvard University

Harvard Yard

Whitneys

Pammy's

Veggie Galaxy

CAMBRIDGE   ● MIT

Charles River

Harvard ② Bridge

Davis Square   Somerville Theatre
Redbones   The Burren

Long Wharf   HARBOR CRU[I]
DOWNTOWN   ①

Fan Pier Park

Barking Crab   Trillium Brewing   Woods Hill Pier 4

Audubon Boston   India Quality
Loretta's Last Call
Game On!   Back Bay Fens
Fenway Park   ④

FENWAY

Museum of Fine Arts

SOUTH END

SOUTH BOSTON

0 km   1
0 miles   1

4 DAYS

Day 1

A relaxing harbor cruise operated by City Experiences (p53) is the ideal way to start your Boston tour and get to know the city from the water. Back on dry land, stroll to the Barking Crab (p103) to grab a tasty lobster roll for lunch. Pause to soak in the skyline views from nearby Fan Pier Park and then make your way to Boston's beloved Trillium Brewing (trilliumbrewing. com) for an IPA flight tasting on the Fort Point property's outdoor patio. End this

Tree-lined Fan Pier Park on Boston's waterfront

waterfront day with a refined dinner on the harbor – Woods Hill Pier 4 (p103), offering locally sourced fare in an elegant setting, is a great choice.

Day 2

Now to venture beyond the city to Cambridge (p124), which sits on the other side of the Charles River. To set foot on Cambridge soil, walk along the river's

---

DRINK
If you need a pick-me-up during your stroll through Cambridge, Veggie Galaxy (www. veggiegalaxy.com) has mastered the art of the vegan frappe, with flavors ranging from peanut butter chocolate to strawberry banana.

> 📷 **VIEW**
> While it seems unassuming at first glance, the Citgo sign towering above Kenmore Square (*p121*) is a beloved Boston landmark and is the backdrop to every Red Sox game at Fenway Park.

most scenic crossing point, the Harvard Bridge – note the bizarre "smoot" measurements marked along the way. Continuing north, you'll arrive at the Massachusetts Institute of Technology (MIT; *p126*) with its landscaped gardens, prestigious museum, and massive Great Dome. Pause for lunch at Pammy's (*p131*), a refined restaurant serving elegant Italian cuisine and wine. Spend the afternoon at Harvard University (*p30*). Tour the Museum of Natural History (*p125*) to see dinosaur skeletons, admire the preserved wildlife, and view the museum's internationally acclaimed collection of glass models of plants, then head to Harvard Yard to explore the bookshops. Celebrate your Cambridge adventure with a beer at Whitneys (*p130*).

Day 3

Today, immerse yourself in the beauty of Massachusetts. Hail a Lyft or Uber to take you to Middlesex Fells, a sprawling green space north of Boston. Hiking trails abound across the area, with the best options for a morning hike being the easy 1.5-mile (2-km) Sheepfold Path Loop, which offers scenic views along the reservoir, or the more challenging 4-mile (7-km) Rock Circuit Trail, perfect for ambitious outdoor adventurers hoping to spot wildlife. After a successful hike, journey down south to Somerville's Davis Square (*p127*) for a well-earned rest and a bite to eat – Redbones (*p131*) is ideal for a hearty lunch of pulled pork and dirty rice. In the evening, catch a show at the Somerville Theatre, and then finish the day with a glass of Irish whiskey and some live music at the Burren (*p130*).

Day 4

Make the most of your final morning with a foray across Fenway (*p118*), a historic Boston neighborhood once dominated by swampland. Wander along the tranquil paths within the Back Bay Fens (*p120*) and then make your way to the Museum of Fine Arts (MFA; *p36*). Spend the rest of the morning exploring this iconic institution, which is home to roughly 500,000 items including works from dynastic Egypt, classical China, France's Impressionist revolution, and the ancient Americas. For lunch, stick close to the MFA to sample classic Southern cuisine and country music at Loretta's Last Call (*p122*). Later, head to Fenway Park (*p119*) to catch a Red Sox game, or watch the match on the screen at Game On! (*p122*), located adjacent to the stadium. For dinner, fire up your taste buds with the spicy offerings at India Quality (*p123*), then pop by Audubon Boston (*p122*) for a masterfully crafted cocktail and a final goodbye to the city.

Fenway Park stadium, home of the Boston Red Sox

TOP 10 HIGHLIGHTS

Boston Common

EXPLORE THE
HIGHLIGHTS

There are some sights in Boston you simply shouldn't miss, and it's these attractions that make the Top 10. Discover what makes each one a must-see on the following pages.

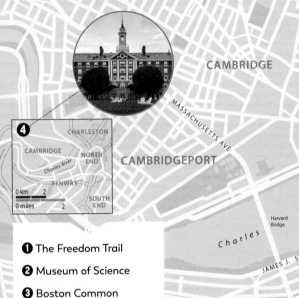

CHARLESTOWN

EAST
CAMBRIDGE

9

North Washington
Street Bridge

2

Leonard P. Zakim
Bunker Hill
Memorial Bridge

Langone
Park

NORTH
END

Charlesbank
Park

WEST
END

Longfellow
Bridge

BEACON
HILL

WATERFRONT

River

FINANCIAL
DISTRICT

10

*Boston
Common*

1 DOWNTOWN

3

MEMORIAL DR

CLARENDON

CHARLES
STREET

ACK
AY

5

BOYLSTON

STREET

STUART
STREET

CHINATOWN

7

AVENUE

COLUMBUS

SOUTH
END

SOUTH
BOSTON

AVENUE

| 0 meters | 500 |
| 0 yards | 500 |

THE FREEDOM TRAIL

📍 P4 🌐 thefreedomtrail.org

From Boston Common to the heights of Bunker Hill, the 2.5-mile (4-km) Freedom Trail traces Boston's fascinating revolutionary history. You can't get lost – simply follow the red stripe on the sidewalk to find the 16 nationally recognized historic landmarks. The map below shows a slightly shortened version of the full route, which extends farther north and across the Charles River.

1 Massachusetts State House

Boston architect Charles Bulfinch's *pièce de résistance*, the "new" State House (completed in 1798) is one of the city's most distinctive buildings (*p85*).

2 Park Street Church

🏠 1 Park St 🌐 park street.org

This church, founded by a small group of Christians disenchanted with their Unitarian-leaning congregation, was dedicated in 1810. Abolitionist William Lloyd Garrison gave his first public antislavery speech here in 1829.

3 Old Granary Burying Ground

A veritable who's-who of revolutionary history lie in this plot (*p105*) next to Park Street Church. One

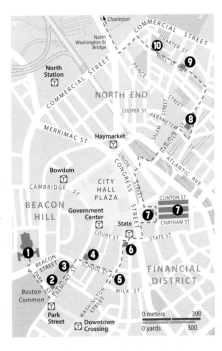

of the most well-known residents here is Samuel Adams (*p50*).

4 King's Chapel

The current granite building (*p106*) dates from around 1749, but the chapel was originally founded in 1686 by King James II as an outpost of the Anglican Church.

Don't miss the burying ground next door, which shelters Massachusetts' first governor, John Winthrop (*p50*).

5 Old South Meeting House

Boston's Old South Meeting House (*p106*) was one of the largest meeting halls in colonial

---

EAT
You are sure to work up an appetite on this walk. Allow time to stop in at one of the Italian cafés and bakeries along Hanover Street in the North End to refuel.

A bronze Freedom Trail marker, one of many lining the sidewalks

Boston, and its rafters often rang with fiery speeches against slavery and for free speech.

6 Old State House

Built in 1713, this stately building (p105), presiding over the head of State Street, was the headquarters of the colonial legislature and the Royal Governor. The Declaration of Independence was first read from its balcony.

7 Faneuil Hall and Quincy Market

Known as the "Cradle of Liberty," Faneuil Hall (p105) has hosted many

The dignified exterior of the Old State House

revolutionary meetings in its time. Neighboring Quincy Market once housed the city's wholesale food distribution.

8 Paul Revere House

In North Square, Paul Revere House (p99) is one of Boston's oldest private residences. Its namesake (p50) was well regarded locally as a metalsmith and engraver prior to his history-changing ride.

9 Old North Church

This church (p99) has a pivotal place in revolutionary history. Prior to his midnight ride, Revere (p50) ordered Robert Newman to hang one or two lamps in the belfry to indicate, respectively, whether the British were approaching by land or via the Charles River.

10 Copp's Hill Burying Ground

This is Boston's second-oldest cemetery after the one by King's Chapel. Established in 1660, Copp's Hill (p99) contains the graves of numerous soldiers of the Revolution.

WALKING THE TRAIL

Maps of the trail are available at the Boston Common Visitor Center, or at the Boston National Park headquarters at Faneuil Hall, where free, ranger-led walking tours are offered. Most of the trail is indicated in red paint with a few sections in red brick. On leaving Boston Common, the first section of the route weaves its way through the central city and Old Boston. Distances begin to stretch out on the second half as the trail meanders through the narrow streets of the North End to Charlestown.

A painting depicting the Battle of Lexington

Moments in Revolutionary History

1. Resistance to the Stamp Act (1765)

The king imposed a stamp duty on all published materials in the colonies, including newspapers. Furious Bostonians boycotted British goods in response.

2. Boston Massacre (1770)

On March 5, in front of the Old State House (p105), an angry mob of colonists taunted British guardsmen with insults, rocks, and snowballs. The soldiers opened fire, killing five. The first man killed was Crispus Attucks, a formerly enslaved man of African and Indigenous descent, who became an important symbol in the Civil Rights movement.

3. Samuel Adams' Tea Tax Speech (1773)

Adams' incendiary speech during a forum at the Old South Meeting House inspired the Boston Tea Party, the most subversive action undertaken yet in the debate over colonial secession.

4. Boston Tea Party (1773)

The city's most famous act of rebellion took place at Griffin's Wharf on December 16. Led by Samuel Adams, the Sons of Liberty boarded three British East India Company ships and dumped their cargo into the Boston Harbor, a watershed moment of colonial defiance.

5. Paul Revere's Ride (1775)

Revere rode to Lexington to warn revolutionaries Samuel Adams and John Hancock that British troops intended to arrest them. One of the bravest acts of the war, it would be immortalized in the Longfellow poem *The Midnight Ride of Paul Revere*.

6. Battle of Lexington (1775)

Revere's ride was followed by the first exchange of fire between American militia, known as Minute Men, and British regulars on Lexington Green. Within weeks, the American Revolution had begun.

7. Battle of Bunker Hill (1775)

The colonists' fortification of Charlestown resulted in a full-scale British attack. Despite their defeat, the colonists' resolve was galvanized by this battle.

8. Washington Takes Command (1775)

George Washington, the Virginia plantation owner and former commander in chief of American forces during Queen Anne's War, assumed command of the Continental Army in Cambridge.

9. Fortification of Dorchester Heights (1776)

Fortifying the mouth of Boston Harbor with a captured cannon, Washington put the Royal Navy under his guns and forced a British retreat from the city.

10. Declaration of Independence (1776)

On July 4, the colonies rejected all allegiance to the British Crown. In Boston, independence was declared from the Royal Governor's headquarters, today known as the Old State House.

Paul Revere (1735–1818), who along with Samuel Adams laid the cornerstone of the Massachusetts State House

The Charles Bulfinch-designed State House, with its striking facade and iconic dome sheathed in 23-carat gold leaf

MASSACHUSETTS STATE HOUSE

The cornerstone of the Massachusetts State House (*p85*) was laid on July 4, 1795, by statesman Samuel Adams and Paul Revere. Finished on January 11, 1798, this is architect Charles Bulfinch's masterwork. With its brash design details, imposing stature, and liberal use of fine materials, it embodies the optimism of post-revolutionary America. The building served as a model for the US Capitol Building in Washington, DC, and as inspiration for other state capitols around the country.

The building is in three distinct sections: the original Bulfinch front; the marble wings constructed in 1917; and the yellow-brick 1895 addition, known as the Brigham Extension after the architect who designed it. Just below Bulfinch's central colonnade, statues of famous Massachusetts figures strike poses. Among them are the great orator Daniel Webster; President John F. Kennedy; and Quaker Mary Dyer, who was hanged in 1660 for challenging the authority of Boston's religious leaders. Directly below the State House's immense gilded dome is the Senate Chamber, site of many influential speeches and debates. The dome serves as the zero-mile marker for Massachusetts, making it, as physician and poet Oliver Wendell Holmes Sr. remarked, "the hub of the universe."

MUSEUM OF SCIENCE

📍 F2 🏛 1 Science Park 🕐 9am–5pm Sat–Thu, 9am–9pm Fri 🌐 mos.org ⟳

With over 700 colorful, interactive displays, covering natural history, astronomy, computing, and the wonders of the physical sciences, it's no surprise that this is one of Boston's most-visited museums. Attractions include a jaw-dropping IMAX® screen, the Hall of Human Life, lightning demonstrations, and live science shows.

1 To the Moon

In this exhibit, peek inside the full-size replicas of the Apollo Command Module and the Lunar Module cockpit to relive the first landing on the moon. Nearby models show the growth of space stations from Skylab and Mir to the International Space Station. Pieces of moon rock are on display as well.

2 Garden Walk and Insect Zoo

A range of plants, including carnivorous plants and local plants that are great for pollinators, are found at this tropical garden. The insect zoo highlights invertebrates such as stick insects, true bugs, tarantulas, and scorpions. Watch the leaf-cutter ants collect leaves for their fungal gardens.

🍽 EAT
Hungry? The museum's Riverview Café (situated on level 1) offers reliably good, reasonably priced food, including burgers, sandwiches, pizzas, and salads.

3 Science Live! Stage

This live presentation features hands-on science demonstrations. Meet an alligator, explore nanotechnology, or find out why our brains fall for optical illusions. A daily changing schedule keeps up with the latest advancements making the news.

4 Discovery Center

Geared to children under eight, this fun, activity-filled center is all about stimulating young minds with a sense of exploration. The changing activities can include excavating artifacts, analyzing fingerprints, or creating slime with borax and school glue. Museum staff help children discover the fun of problem-solving.

Key to Floor Plan
- ▩ Level 2
- ▩ Level 1
- ▩ Lower Level

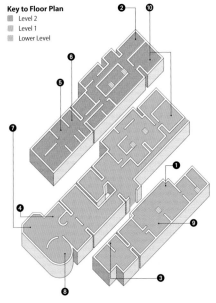

Museum of Science Floor Plan

The Van de Graaff generator in the Lightning! theatre

5 Hall of Human Life

Designed to revolutionize how visitors engage with their own biology and manage their health, the exhibits in this hall explore cutting-edge subjects such as GMO research, DNA sequencing, the function of the human body, and all sorts of medical and nutritional issues. Visitors are given a barcode wristband that records their responses to more than 70 different challenges and activities.

MUSEUM HISTORY

The Boston Museum of Science (MOS) traces its origins to the founding of the Boston Society of Natural History in 1830. The first permanent museum opened in 1864 in Back Bay, making MOS one of the oldest science museums in America. The museum moved to its current location in 1951.

6 Project Vaccine

Learn about the science and people responsible for vaccine development and investigate how the human immune system works. Explore varied viewpoints and ask experts questions.

7 Charles Hayden Planetarium

This notable high-tech planetarium brings the dazzling night sky to life, and presents daily shows, ranging from exhibitions on NASA's latest space missions to a kid-themed exploration of the stars with Sesame Street's Big Bird and Elmo.

8 Mugar Omni Theater

This remarkable five-story IMAX® theater takes the concept of the "big-screen" to a whole new level. Sit below a 180-degree dome that fills your entire range of vision, immersing your senses with spectacular moving images and powerful digital sounds.

9 Colossal Fossil

Meet Cliff, one of only four nearly complete triceratops skeletons on display in the world. He looks pretty good considering he's 65 million years old. Discovered in North Dakota in 2004, Cliff measures 23 ft (7 m) from horn tip to tail, and his head alone weighs 800 lb (362 kg).

Cliff, the museum's huge triceratops skeleton

10 Lightning!

This live-theater show explores electricity. Its star is the air-insulated Van de Graaff generator, which safely zaps out sizzling lightning bolts of up to 1 million volts.

BOSTON COMMON AND PUBLIC GARDEN

📍 M4, N4 ℹ️ 139 Tremont St; boston.gov/parks/boston-common

These two adjacent urban oases form part of Boston's Emerald Necklace. Boston Common, once a grazing pasture, is a much-loved green space and a focal point of the city. The Public Garden exudes charm, with its sinuous paths and weeping willows. In summertime its lagoon is dotted with swan boats – an iconic image of Boston.

1 Frog Pond
During summer, kids enjoy the iridescent spray of the pond's fountains. Come winter, Bostonians of all ages take to the ice. Skate rentals and hot chocolate are nearby.

2 Lagoon Bridge
This elegant faux suspension bridge crossing the Public Garden lagoon has served as the romantic setting for numerous wedding photos.

3 Parkman Bandstand
Built in 1912 to honor George Parkman, a benefactor of the park, this elegant bandstand is modeled on Versailles' *Temple d'Amour* (temple of love). It hosts everything from concerts to political rallies.

4 Shaw Memorial
Augustus Saint-Gaudens' lifelike bronze pays homage to the "Fighting 54th" – one of the only entirely African American regiments in the Civil War. Led by Boston-born Robert Shaw, the 54th displayed great battle valor.

5 Bronze of George Washington
Created by local sculptor Thomas Ball in 1869, this colossal bronze statue was an early horseback depiction of George Washington in midlife, before he became the nation's first president.

6 Soldiers and Sailors Monument
Over 25,000 Union Army veterans remembered

☕ **DRINK**
No matter the weather, grab warm and cold drinks from the Frog Pond Café. Ice cream is also offered here, perfect for hot summer days.

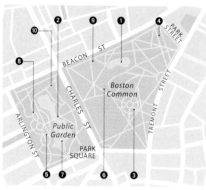

Leafy Boston Common, overlooked by buildings

their fallen Civil War comrades at the 1877 dedication of Martin Milmore's impressive memorial. Bas-reliefs depict the soldiers' and sailors' departure to and return from war.

EMERALD NECKLACE

Frederick Law Olmsted, designer of New York's Central Park, created parks in Boston to solve environmental problems and provide refuges for the locals. The 7-mile (11-km) Emerald Necklace includes Boston Common, the Public Garden, Back Bay Fens, Commonwealth Avenue Mall, Jamaica Pond, the Riverway, Arnold Arboretum, and Franklin Park.

7 Swan Boats

Summer hasn't officially arrived in Boston until the iconic swan boats emerge from hibernation in mid-April and glide onto the Public Garden lagoon. The swans, with their arched necks and brilliantly painted bills, can each accommodate up to 20 people.

8 Ether Monument

This 1868 statue and fountain commemorates a groundbreaking operation conducted under general anesthesia by ether at Massachusetts General Hospital in 1846 (p57). This is a rare monument to the powers of a drug.

9 Founders' Memorial

John F. Paramino's 1930 bronze depicts William Blaxton, Boston's first English settler, greeting John Winthrop (p50).

10 Make Way for Ducklings Statuettes

Eight little ducklings seem to have sprung from the pages of Robert McCloskey's much-loved kids' book *Make Way for Ducklings* and fallen in line behind their mother at the lagoon's edge.

Make Way for Ducklings, by Nancy Schön

HARVARD UNIVERSITY

📍 B1–C1 ℹ️ 1350 Massachusetts Ave; harvard.edu ☑️

America's most prestigious university, founded in 1636, has touched every corner of American cultural, political, professional, and business life. Eight American presidents – most recently Barack Obama and George W. Bush – and the heads of state of another 18 nations, as well as 48 Nobel laureates, and 44 winners of the Pulitzer Prize, number among its faculty and alumni.

1 Massachusetts Hall

Constructed in 1720, the university's oldest building was once a barrack for 640 revolutionary soldiers. The hall houses the office of the President of Harvard and is usually the center of protests against university policies.

2 Harvard Art Museums

With works of art ranging from the ancient world to the present day, the Harvard Art Museums bring together the collections of the university's three art museums (p125). Exhibits include European and American art of the Fogg Museum, Germanic art holdings of the Busch-Reisinger Museum, and Asian artworks of the Sackler Museum.

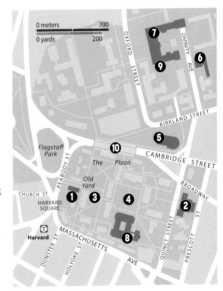

The Lamentation over the Dead Christ, Fogg Museum

3 John Harvard Statue

This statue's inscription states "John Harvard, Founder 1638," hence the statue's nickname "The Statue of Three Lies." First, there is no known portrait of John Harvard, so the sculptor used a model; second, Harvard did not found the university – it was named after him; and third, it was founded in 1636, not 1638.

4 Harvard Yard

Harvard's mixed residential and academic yard became the standard by which most American institutions of higher learning modeled their campuses.

5 Memorial Hall

Built over eight years, Harvard's Memorial Hall pays tribute to Harvard's Union casualties from the Civil War. It was officially opened in 1878. This

Strolling through Harvard University's campus

multipurpose building has hosted theatrical performances, graduation exercises, and assemblies of many other kinds.

6 Museum of the Ancient Near East

⌂ 6 Divinity Ave
🕐 11am–4pm Sun–Fri
Founded in 1889, this museum houses more than 40,000 objects from excavations in Egypt, Iraq, Israel, Jordan, Syria, and Tunisia.

7 Museum of Natural History

This is actually three brilliant museums rolled into one: the Museum of Comparative Zoology, the Mineralogical and Geological Museum, and the Herbaria. The exhibits here *(p125)* include a trio of whale skeletons

hanging from the ceiling, a Brazilian amethyst geode, a mounted Kronosaurus skeleton, and glass flowers – 780 species of plants, painstakingly replicated in colorful glass.

8 Harry Widener Memorial Library

The Widener is the largest university library in the US. It houses an impressive collection of rare books, including a Gutenberg Bible and early editions of Shakespeare's collected works. Access to the library is only possible if accompanied by someone with valid Harvard ID.

9 Peabody Museum of Archaeology and Ethnology

With an extensive collection, this museum *(p125)* features a permanent Mesoamerica exhibit, Encounters with the Americas exploring Latin American culture, and an exhibition that is devoted to canoes

created by the Penobscot people of Maine.

10 Science Center Plaza

This plaza in front of the Undergraduate Science Center is Harvard's busiest social space. It's home to the Tanner Fountain, benches, and food trucks.

ACKNOWLEDGING THE PAST

In 2017, Harvard Law School marked its bicentennial by dedicating a plaque to honor the enslaved people whose labor created the wealth on which the school was founded. "May we pursue the highest ideals of law and justice in their memory," it reads. Harvard is one of many universities – including Brown and Georgetown – struggling with historical ties to the trade of enslaved people.

Harvard Alumni

1. John Adams (1735–1826)
The nation's second president, although nervous upon entering the illustrious college as a freshman, eventually became enthralled by his studies.

2. W. E. B. Du Bois (1868–1963)
Founder of the National Association for the Advancement of Colored People (NAACP), Du Bois studied philosophy here, and said of his experience, "I was in Harvard, but not of it."

3. Franklin Delano Roosevelt (1882–1945)
Apparently more of a social butterfly than a dedicated academic, F.D.R. played pranks, led the freshman football squad, edited the *Harvard Crimson*, and earned a C average at Harvard before going on to become the 32nd president of the United States.

4. John F. Kennedy (1917–63)
A barely average student but a good athlete, John F. Kennedy ran for president of the freshman class in 1936, and lost badly. He did rather well in 1960 when he became the 35th president of the United States.

5. Leonard Bernstein (1918–90)
The country's greatest composer and conductor was firmly grounded in the arts at Harvard. He edited the *Advocate*, the college's estimable literary and performing arts journal.

6. Margaret Atwood (b. 1939)
Distinguished poet and author Margaret Atwood received a master's degree in 1962 from Radcliffe College, a private women's college that fully merged with Harvard in 1999. Post-graduation, she went on to pen *The Handmaid's Tale*, a dystopian novel that's renowned for its exploration of feminist themes.

Composer Leonard Bernstein conducting an orchestra

7. Benazir Bhutto (1953–2007)
This class of 1973 alumna later became the first woman to lead a modern Muslim state when she was elected prime minister of Pakistan in 1988. She was assassinated in 2007.

8. Bill Gates (b. 1955)
William Henry Gates III dropped out of Harvard in his third year to found Microsoft. He was made an Honorary Knight Commander of the Order of the British Empire (KBE) by Queen Elizabeth II in 2005 for his humanitarian and philanthropic work. He was also awarded an honorary doctorate in 2007 by Harvard.

9. Barack Obama (b. 1961)
The 44th president of the United States attended Harvard Law School in 1988–91. His election as the first Black president of the *Harvard Law Review* gained extensive media attention.

10. Natalie Portman (b. 1981)
Actor Natalie Portman, known for films such as *Closer*, *V for Vendetta*, and *Black Swan*, completed an undergraduate degree at Harvard, ultimately earning a bachelor's degree in psychology in 2003.

HARVARD'S "ARCHITECTURAL ZOO"

Swiss-French architect Le Corbusier

Modernist architect James Stirling described Harvard as an "architectural zoo" – a well-deserved moniker as the campus seems to include buildings designed by every prominent architect of the last 200 years. Stirling himself designed the modernist 1985 Sackler Museum building. Charles Bulfinch, whose claim to fame is the Massachusetts State House *(p85)*, contributed the 1814 University Hall, featuring an ingenious granite staircase that supports the building by virtue of its interlocking steps. Walter Gropius, the Bauhaus founder and Harvard architecture professor (1937–52), designed the Harvard Graduate Center in 1950, as well as several dormitory complexes. Gropius strove to make his modernist projects seem welcoming for inhabitants, but industrial finishes have not always resonated with succeeding generations. Le Corbusier, widely acknowledged as one of the pioneers of the modernist movement, designed the Carpenter Center for Visual Arts. This building is a lyrical collection of forms, materials, and innovative curves, with entire walls made of glass and deeply grooved concrete.

Carpenter Center for Visual Arts, an example of Le Corbusier's work

AROUND NEWBURY STREET

📍 K5, L5, M5

You'll see some of the best-dressed Bostonians along Newbury Street, where many ready-to-wear boutiques cater to couture-conscious style. But don't let the profusion of fashionistas fool you: there's much more to elegant Newbury Street than world-class retail and some of the city's best sidewalk dining. Look closely and you'll glimpse a historical side to Newbury Street all but unseen by the shoppers.

1 Emmanuel Church

🏠 15 Newbury St

Architect Alexander Estey's impressive church (1860) was the first building to grace Newbury after the infilling of Back Bay. The adjacent Lindsey Chapel (1924) is home to the renowned Emmanuel Music ensemble.

TOP TIP

View the schedule for Emmanuel Music online (emmanuel music.org).

2 French Cultural Center

🏠 53 Marlborough St

🕐 Hours vary, chech web-site 🌐 frenchlibrary.org

Housed in a grand Back Bay mansion, the French Cultural Center hosts everything from lectures and courses in French to concerts and a tasteful Bastille Day celebration.

3 Church of the Covenant

🏠 67 Newbury St

Architect Richard Upjohn left his Neo-Gothic mark on Boston with the Church of the Covenant (1865). It has one of the world's largest collection of Tiffany stained glass.

4 Kingsley Montessori School

🏠 26 Exeter St

🚫 To the public

Originally built as a Spiritualist temple in 1884, this building became the dignified Exeter Street Theater in 1914. In 2005, it was converted to a private school.

5 Commonwealth Avenue

A mall running along the center of Commonwealth Avenue (p92) provides a leafy respite from the Newbury Street throngs. Benches and a number of bronze sculptures

Newbury Street, Boston's main shopping street

of historical figures line the pedestrian path. The Boston Women's Memorial here honors First Lady Abigail Adams, abolitionist and suffragist Lucy Stone, and Phillis Wheatley, the first formerly enslaved woman in the US to publish a book of poetry.

6 New England Historic Genealogical Society

🏠 101 Newbury St 🕐 By appointment, chech website 🌐 american ancestors.org

Members seek to discover more about their New England progenitors in one of the most extensive genealogical libraries in the US.

🍴 EAT
After a morning of shopping, buy picnic supplies at Deluca's Bach Bay Marhet (*329 Newbury St*) and head to Boston Public Garden (*p28*) to recuperate.

7 Gibson House Museum

One of Back Bay's first private homes, Gibson House was also one of the most modern residences of its day (*p92*). With its gas lighting, indoor plumbing, and heating, it spurred a building boom in the area.

8 Trinity Church Rectory

🏠 233 Clarendon St
🚫 To the public

H. H. Richardson, principal architect of Trinity Church (*p40*), was commissioned to build this rectory in 1879. His work echoes the Romanesque Revival style of the Copley Square church.

9 Boston Architectural College

🏠 320 Newbury St
🕐 For tours and events, chech website
🌐 the-bac.edu

Since 1889, aspiring architects have studied at this college. The McCormick Gallery hosts a number of changing exhibitions.

10 234 Berkeley St

Originally a natural history museum opened in 1864, this landmark building is now the location of a high-end home furnishings store.

Clockwise from right **Emmanuel Church; a window in the Church of the Covenant; statue on Commonwealth Avenue; the red study room, Gibson House Museum**

MUSEUM OF FINE ARTS, BOSTON

📍 D6 🏛 Avenue of the Arts, 465 Huntington Ave 🕐 10am–5pm Wed–Sun (to 10pm Thu & Fri) 🌐 mfa.org 🖋🗺

Since it was founded in 1870, the **Museum of Fine Arts (MFA)** has collected around 500,000 pieces from an array of cultures and civilizations, ranging from ancient Egyptian tomb treasures to cutting-edge contemporary artworks. This is the largest art museum in New England and one of the great encyclopedic art museums in the US.

1 The Fog Warning

This late 19th-century painting by Winslow Homer is part of a series in which the artist portrayed the difficult lives of the local fishers and their families. The painting depicts a fisherman trying to return to his vessel.

2 John Singleton Copley Portraits

Self-taught and Boston-born Copley gained fame by painting the most affluent and influential Bostonians of his day, including figures like John Hancock, John Adams, and Isaac Winslow, who is depicted alongside his wife.

3 Silverwork by Paul Revere

Famed for his midnight ride, Paul Revere *(p50)*

TOP TIP

The MFA offers family activities to inspire little ones; check the website.

was also known for his masterful silverwork. The breadth of his ability in this craft is clearly apparent in the museum's magnificent 200-piece collection.

4 Sargent Murals

Having secured some of John Singer Sargent's most important portrai-ture in the early 20th century, the MFA went one step further and commissioned the artist to paint murals and bas-reliefs on its central rotunda and colonnade.

The exquisite Egyptian Royal Pectoral

They feature gods and heroes from classical mythology.

5 Dance at Bougival

This endearing image (1883) of a young couple dancing is one of the most beloved of Renoir's works. It exemplifies the artist's knack for taking a timeless situation and making it contemporary by dressing his subjects in the latest fashions.

Admiring works at the Museum of Fine Arts

6 Egyptian Royal Pectoral

An extremely rare chest ornament, this pectoral is nearly 4,000 years old. A vulture with a cobra on its left wing is depicted, poised to strike.

7 Christ in Majesty with Symbols

Acquired in 1919 from a small Spanish church, this medieval fresco had an amazingly complex journey to Boston, which involved waterproofing it with lime and parmesan for safe transportation.

8 La Japonaise

Claude Monet's 1876 portrait reflects a time when Japanese culture fascinated Europe's most style-conscious circles. The model, interestingly, is Monet's wife, Camille.

9 Japanese Temple Room

With its wood paneling and subdued lighting, the Temple Room evokes ancient Japanese shrines atop mist-enshrouded mountains. The statues, which date from as early as the 7th century, depict prominent figures from Buddhist texts.

10 Statue of King Aspelta

This statue of the 6th-century BCE Nubian king, Aspelta, was recovered in 1920 at Nuri in present-day Sudan during a Museum of Fine Arts/ Harvard joint expedition.

Christ in Majesty with Symbols fresco

Museum of Fine Arts Collections

Japanese Edo-period print on display in the MFA's Art of Asia collection

1. Art of Asia

For Asian art connoisseurs, the museum offers a dizzying overview of Japan's multiple artistic forms. In fact, the MFA holds the largest collection of ancient Japanese art outside of Japan. In addition to the tranquil Temple Room (p37), with its centuries-old Buddhist statues, visitors should look out for the beautiful hanging scrolls and woodblock prints, with their dramatic landscapes and spirited renderings of everyday life. Kurasawa fans, meanwhile, will be enthralled by the menacing samurai weaponry. Additionally, the Art of Asia collection contains exquisite objects from 2,000 years of Chinese, Indian, and Southeast Asian history, including sensuous ivory figurines, pictorial carpets, and vibrant watercolors.

2. Classical Art

The remarkable Classical Art collection has a hoard of gold bracelets, glass, mosaic bowls, and stately marble busts. One of the earliest pieces is a c. 1500 BCE gold axe, inscribed with symbols from a still-undeciphered Cretan language.

3. Art of the Americas

The MFA's Art of the Americas wing, designed by Norman Foster, opened in 2010. The wing features pieces dating from pre-Columbian times, through to the first quarter of the 21st century, and showcases about 5,000 works produced in North, Central, and South America. The museum has profited from generous benefactors over the years and the collection holds the world's finest ensemble of colonial New England furniture, rare 17th-century American portraiture, a superb display of American silver, and paintings by the country's own "Old" Masters, including Copley, Stuart, Cole, Sargent, Cassat, Homer, and many others.

4. Textile and Fashion Arts

Rotating displays highlight pictorial quilts, period fashions, fine Persian rugs, and pre-contact Andean weavings. Particularly interesting are the textiles and costumes from the Elizabethan and Stuart periods – an unprecedented 1943 donation from the private collection of Elizabeth Day McCormick.

Stuart woman's doublet, dating from 1610–15

An exhibit showcasing the MFA's musical instruments

5. Musical Instruments
Priceless 17th-century guitars, ornately inlaid pianos, and even a mouth organ are on view to visitors of the MFA. Among the more distinctive pieces is a c. 1796 English grand piano – the earliest extant example of a piano with a six-octave range – and a 1680 French guitar by the Voboam workshop.

6. Art of Egypt, Nubia, and the Ancient Near East
This collection is a treasure trove of millennia-old Egyptian sarcophagi, tomb finds, and Nubian jewelry and objects from everyday life. The assemblage of Egyptian funerary pieces, including beautifully crafted jewelry and ceramic urns, is quite awe-inspiring. Ancient Near Eastern objects, with their bold iconography and rich materials, illustrate why the region is known as the Cradle of Civilization.

7. European Art to 1900
From 12th-century tempera baptism paintings to Claude Monet's *Haystacks*, the MFA's European collection is staggeringly diverse. Painstakingly transferred medieval stained-glass windows, beautifully illuminated Bibles, and delicate French tapestries are displayed alongside works by Old Masters: Titian, El Greco, Rembrandt, and Rubens. A superlative Impressionist and Post-Impressionist collection features masterpieces from the likes of Renoir, Degas, Cézanne, and Van Gogh, plus the finest group of Monet's works outside of Paris.

8. Contemporary Art
Given Boston's affinity for the traditional, you might be surprised by this world-class collection of contemporary and late 20th-century art. It includes works by the painter and photographer Chuck Close and the Abstract Expressionist artist Jackson Pollock, which are on display in the Art of the Americas wing. New Media is also well represented here.

9. Art of Africa and Oceania
Artifacts from these collections include Melanese canoe ornaments, dramatic Congolese bird sculptures, and African funerary art. The most popular African displays are the powerful-looking 19th- and 20th-century wooden masks.

10. "Please be Seated!" Installations
View (and sit on) one of the country's most comprehensive collections of American contemporary furniture. The museum encourages visitors to admire and sit on these furniture pieces, so take a break and have a seat on fine American handiwork by designers such as Maloof, Castle, and Eames.

La Berceuse (1889) by Van Gogh, part of the European Art collection

TRINITY CHURCH

📍 L5 🏠 206 Clarendon St ⏰ 10am–5pm Wed–Sat, for services Sun
🌐 trinitychurchboston.org 🔗🔗

Boston has a great knack for creating curious visual juxtapositions, and one of the most remarkable is in Copley Square. Henry Hobson Richardson's 19th-century Trinity Church contrasts with the sleek, blue-tinted glass of the modern and imposing 200 Clarendon Tower.

1 The Foundation
As part of Richardson's daring plan for the new Trinity Church, the first of 4,500 wooden support pilings for the building was driven into the soggy Back Bay landfill in 1873. Reverend Phillips Brooks laid the cornerstone two years later.

SHOP
Items in the on-site shop have designs inspired by the decorative details of the church. The bookmarks make lovely souvenirs.

2 Front Facade and Side Towers
The Romanesque church of St Trophime in Arles, France, was Richardson's inspiration when he redesigned Trinity's front portico, along with its two new side towers. The additions were put in place by his firm of architects in the 1890s, after his death in 1886.

3 Central Tower
The church's central tower borrows its square design from the New Cathedral of Salamanca, in Spain. Inside, vibrant wall paintings by La Farge depicting biblical figures stand in sharp contrast to the normally austere church interiors of the artist's day.

4 Embroidered Kneelers
Trinity's colorful kneelers have been stitched by parishioners in memory of people and events past. They serve as an informal folk history of the congregation.

5 Pulpit Carving
Preachers from throughout the ages, including St. Paul, Martin Luther, and

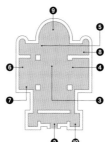

Trinity Church Floor Plan

7 La Farge Windows

A newcomer to stained glasswork at the time, John La Farge approached his commissions, such as the breathtaking *Christ in Majesty*, with the same sense of daring and vitality that architect Richardson employed in his Trinity design.

8 Phillips Brooks' Bust

Keeping watch over the baptismal font is Rector Brooks. Renowned for his bold sermons, he was a rector at Trinity from 1869 to 1891.

9 The Chancel

On the wall of the chancel are a series of seven gold bas-reliefs that depict figures from the history of Christianity. The striking marble altar was added in 1938.

10 Organ Pipes

The beautiful organ pipes frame the church's west wall. Exquisitely designed, ornately painted, and – of course – extremely sonorous, the pipes seem to hug the church's ceiling arches.

Trinity Church, next to 200 Clarendon Tower

TOP TIP

From September to June, organ recitals are held on Fridays, 12:15–12:45pm.

Phillips Brooks of Trinity, are depicted in high relief on the pulpit designed by Charles Coolidge.

6 Burne-Jones Windows

Edward Burne-Jones' windows – on the Boylston Street side – were inspired by the burgeoning English Arts and Crafts Movement. Its influence is readily apparent in his *David's Charge to Solomon*, with its bold patterning and rich colors.

TRINITY SINGS "HALLELUJAH"

One of Boston's most cherished traditions is the singing of Handel's *Messiah*, with its unmistakable and rousing "Hallelujah Chorus," at Trinity during the Christmas season. Hundreds pack the sanctuary to experience the choir's ethereal, masterful treatment of the piece. Check the website for details of the performance.

Striking interior of Trinity Church

ISABELLA STEWART GARDNER MUSEUM

📍 D6   🏠 25 Evans Way   🕐 11am–5pm Wed–Mon (to 9pm Thu)
🌐 gardnermuseum.org 🔗🔗

You don't need to be an art lover to be wowed by the Gardner Museum. Its namesake traveled tirelessly to acquire a world-class art collection, which is housed in a Venetian-style palazzo where flowers bloom, sculpted nudes pose in corners, and ceilings reveal their European origins.

1 Titian Room
The museum's most significant gallery was conceived by Gardner as the palazzo's grand reception hall. It has an Italian flavor and showcases Cillini's *Bindo Altoviti* and Titian's *Rape of Europa*, which is considered to be the best of Titian's work in a US museum.

2 The Courtyard
Gardner integrated Roman, Byzantine, Romanesque, Gothic, and Renaissance elements in the magnificent courtyard. It's out of bounds for visitors but can be viewed through the graceful arches surrounding it.

3 Long Gallery
Roman sculptural fragments and busts line glass cases that are filled with unusual 15th- and 16th-century books and artifacts. One such rare tome is a 1481 copy of Dante's *The Divine Comedy*, which features drawings by Botticelli. Also here are items of furniture from the 17th and 18th centuries.

> **TOP TIP**
>
> The museum offers free admission for anyone named Isabella.

4 Tapestry Room
Restored to its original 1914 state, this sweeping gallery houses two 16th-century Belgian tapestry cycles: one depicting *Scenes from the Life of*

Artworks on display in the Blue Room

Cyrus the Great and the other *Scenes from the Life of Abraham*.

5 Dutch Room

Housing some of Gardner's most impressive Dutch and Flemish paintings, this room lost a Vermeer and three Rembrandts in a 1990 art heist that remains unsolved. The museum still offers $10 million for information leading to the recovery of its stolen artworks.

6 Macknight, Yellow, and Blue Rooms

The Macknight, Yellow, and Blue rooms house portraits and sketches by Gardner's contemporaries such as Manet, Matisse, Degas, and Sargent. Of particular note is Sargent's *Mrs Gardner in White*.

7 Gothic Room

John Singer Sargent's masterful and revealing 1888 portrait of Isabella Stewart Gardner is here, as well as medieval liturgical artwork from the 13th century.

Isabella Stewart Gardner Museum's courtyard

Isabella Stewart Gardner Museum Floor Plan

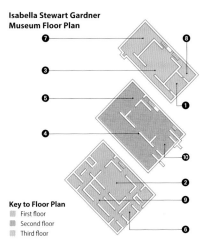

Key to Floor Plan
- First floor
- Second floor
- Third floor

8 Veronese Room

With its richly gilded and painted Spanish-leather wall coverings, it's easy to miss this gallery's highlight: look up at Paolo Veronese's 16th-century masterwork *The Coronation of Hebe*.

9 Spanish Cloister

With stunning mosaic tiling and a Moorish arch, the Spanish Cloister looks like a hidden patio at the Alhambra. But Sargent's sweeping *El Jaleo* (1882), all sultry shadows and rich hues, gives the room its distinctiveness.

10 Raphael Room

Gardner was the first collector to bring works by Raphael to the US; three of his major works are here, alongside Botticelli's *Tragedy of Lucretia* and Crivelli's *St. George Slaying the Dragon*.

"MRS. JACK"

In the 19th century, Isabella Stewart Gardner, wife of John "Jack" Lowell Gardner Jr., turned her wealth to collecting art, acquiring a notable collection of Old Masters and Italian Renaissance pieces. Her will stipulated that her collection should remain assembled as she originally intended. She believed that works of art should be displayed in a setting that would fire the imagination, so the collection is arranged to enhance the viewing of the items. To encourage visitors to respond to the artworks, many of the objects are left unlabeled, as Gardner had requested.

CHARLESTOWN NAVY YARD

📍 H2 🌐 nps.gov/bost

Some of the most storied battleships in American naval history began life at Charlestown Navy Yard. Established in 1800 as one of the country's first naval yards, Charlestown remained vital to US security until its decommissioning in 1974. From the wooden-hulled USS *Constitution* to the World War II steel destroyer USS *Cassin Young*, the yard gives visitors an all-hands-on-deck historical experience.

1 Navy Yard Visitor Center

🏛 Building 5 ⏰ Hours vary, chech website

Begin your stroll through the yard at the visitor center, where you can find out about the site's many attractions and check on tour schedules.

2 USS Constitution

⏰ Hours vary, chech website; photo ID required for adults 📷

First tested in action during the War of 1812, the USS *Constitution* is the world's oldest warship still afloat. It won 42 battles, lost none, and was never boarded by an enemy. On July 4, a tugboat helps the ship perform an annual turnaround cruise.

EAT

Try some pub grub at the historic Warren Tavern (*warrentavern.com*), a rustic Charlestown institution that dates bach to the 1780s.

---

3 USS Cassin Young

Never defeated, despite withstanding multiple kamikaze bomber-attacks in the Pacific, this World War II era destroyer could be considered USS *Constitution's* 20th-century successor.

4 Ropewalk

This quarter-mile-(0.5-km-) long building (1837) houses steam-powered machinery that produced rope rigging for the nation's warships.

USS *Constitution*, a wooden-hulled warship

5 Bunker Hill Monument

This 220-ft (67-m) granite obelisk has towered over Charlestown waterfront since 1842. It was built to commemorate the first pitched battle of the American Revolution.

6 Dry Dock 1

To facilitate hull repairs to ships, Dry Dock 1 was opened in 1833. It was drained by massive steam-powered pumps.

Dry Dock 1, a vast three-sided granite basin

7 Commandant's House

The oldest building in the yard, dating from 1805, housed the commandants of the First Naval District. With its harbor views and wrap-around veranda, this mansion was ideal for entertaining dignitaries.

8 USS Constitution Museum

⏱ 10am–5pm daily

With activities to keep kids entertained, as well as enough nautical trivia and artifacts to satisfy a naval historian, this museum brings to life USS *Constitution*'s two centuries of service.

9 Muster House

This octagonal brick building was designed in the Georgian Revival style popular in the northeast in the mid-19th century. The house served as an administration hub, where the yard's clerical work was carried out.

10 Marine Railway

The Navy Yard has constantly evolved to meet ever-changing demands and developments. The marine railway was built in 1918 to haul submarines and other vessels out of the water for hull repairs.

OLD IRONSIDES

USS *Constitution* earned its nickname "Old Ironsides" due to the ship's 25-inch-(63-cm-) thick hull at the waterline. Pitted against HMS *Guerriere* during the War of 1812, the ship engaged in a shoot-out that left *Guerriere* all but destroyed. Seeing British cannon balls "bouncing" off USS *Constitution*'s hull, a sailor allegedly exclaimed, "Huzzah! Her sides are made of iron." The rest is history.

NEW ENGLAND AQUARIUM

📍 R3 🏛 Central Wharf 🕐 9am–5pm daily (Jun–Aug: to 6pm) 🌐 neaq.org ↗

The sea pervades nearly every aspect of Boston life, so it's only natural that the New England Aquarium is one of the city's most popular attractions. What sets this aquarium apart is its commitment not only to create an exciting environment to learn about marine life, but also to conserve the natural habitats of its thousands of gilled, feathered, and whiskered inhabitants.

1 Yawkey Coral Reef Center

At the top of the Giant Ocean Tank, this exhibit reveals a close-up look at species found inhabiting the coral reefs of the Caribbean, including long-spined sea urchins and gently swaying garden eels.

2 Penguin Exhibit

Two species of penguins – southern rockhoppers and African – coexist here, frolicking on the central island and taking dips in the pool.

3 Indo-Pacific Coral Reef

This immersive exhibit features floor-to-ceiling tanks filled with artificial coral and brightly colored inhabitants such as blue-striped cleaner fish and mandarinfish.

EAT
Enjoy the local catch at Legal Sea Foods Long Wharf (*legalseafoods.com*), located on the harborfront just a few steps from the aquarium.

4 Atlantic Harbor Seal Exhibit

Harbor seals swim, feed, and play in specially designed tanks outside the aquarium. All have either been born in captivity or rescued and deemed unfit for release into the wild.

A fish in Yawkey Coral Reef Center

Key to Floor Plan
- First floor
- Second floor
- Third floor

**New England Aquarium
Floor Plan**

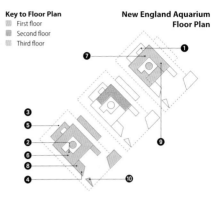

**Giant Ocean Tank, New
England Aquarium**

5 Marine Mammal Center

Observe northern fur seals as they frolic in an open-air exhibit at the edge of the Boston Harbor. Meet the seals and sea lions face-to-face at the large observation deck.

6 Blue Planet Action Center

Interactive exhibits in this section focus on the aquarium's ecological missions: saving corals from climate change and acidification, protecting the critically endangered North Atlantic right whale, as well as promoting sustainable fishing practices.

7 Giant Ocean Tank

Displaying a spectacular four-story Caribbean reef, the Giant Ocean Tank teems with sea turtles, rays, moray eels, tropical fish, and scores of other species in its 200,000-gallon (900,000-liter) space. A curving walkway runs around the outside of the tank from top to bottom and provides viewpoints of the interior of the tank from different levels.

8 Science of Sharks

Wrap around video screens and educational exhibits introduce visitors to these fascinating creatures and their underwater world. This section of the aquarium also has some tanks containing smaller shark species.

9 Gulf of Maine

This six-tank exhibit shows New England's marine and seashore environments inhabited by giant sea stars, sharp-clawed crustaceans, and cold water fish such as cod, halibut, and dogfish.

10 Whale Watch

Swift and stable whale watch catamarans, running mid-March to mid-November, offer a unique glimpse into the life cycles of the world's largest mammals. The swift boats voyage far outside Boston Harbor to the Stellwagen Bank, a prime feeding area for whales.

THE AQUARIUM'S MISSION

The aquarium's aim, first and foremost, is to inspire and support marine conservation. Its Marine Conservation Action Fund has fought on behalf of endangered marine animals worldwide, helping to protect humpback whales in the South Pacific, sea turtles in New England, and dolphins in Peru.

TOP 10 OF EVERYTHING

Boston's Quincy Market

FIGURES IN BOSTON'S HISTORY

1 John Winthrop (1587–1649)

Acting on a daring plan put together by English Puritans in 1629, John Winthrop led approximately 800 people to the Americas to create a settlement in line with their beliefs. He moved his Puritan charges from Charlestown to Boston in 1630 (p8) and served as governor of the Massachusetts Bay Colony until his death.

2 Samuel Adams (1722–1803)

Failed businessman Samuel Adams became Boston's master politician in the eventful years leading up to the Revolution (p9). Adams signed the Declaration of Independence and served in both of the Continental Congresses. He later became the governor of Massachusetts, and joined Paul Revere to lay the cornerstone of the State House (p85) in 1795.

3 Paul Revere (1735–1818)

Best known for his "midnight ride" to forewarn the rebels of the British march on Concord, Revere served the American Revolution as organizer, messenger, and propagandist. A gifted silversmith with many pieces in the Museum of Fine Arts (p36), he founded the metalworking firm that gilded the State House dome and sheathed the hull of the USS Constitution.

4 Margaret Fuller (1810–50)

Tireless advocate for women's rights and education, as well as a campaigner for prison reform and the emancipation of enslaved persons in the US, Fuller was also editor of The Dial, the principal transcendentalist magazine. She served as a war correspondent in Europe and died when her ship sank while coming back to the US.

Samuel Adams, one of the signatories to the Declaration of Independence

5 Donald McKay (1810–80)

McKay built the largest and swiftest of the great clipper ships in his East Boston shipyard in 1850. The speedy vessels revolutionized long-distance shipping at the time of the California Gold Rush and gave Boston its last glory days as a mercantile port before the rise of rail transportation.

6 Mary Baker Eddy (1821–1910)

After recovering from a major accident, Eddy wrote Science and Health with Key to the Scriptures, the basis of Christian Science. She founded a church in Boston in 1879, and in 1892 reorganized it as the First Church of Christ, Scientist. Eddy also established the Pulitzer prize-winning Christian Science Monitor newspaper in 1908.

7 James Michael Curley (1874–1958)

Self-proclaimed champion of "the little people," Curley used patronage and Irish pride to retain a stranglehold on Boston politics from his election as mayor in 1914 until his defeat at the polls in 1949. Known as "the rascal king," he embodied political corruption but created many enduring public works.

8 John F. Kennedy (1917–63)
Grandson of Irish American mayor John "Honey Fitz" Fitzgerald and son of ambassador Joseph Kennedy, John F. Kennedy represented Boston in both houses of the US Congress before he became the first Roman Catholic elected president of the United States. The presidential library *(p135)* at Columbia Point recounts the story of his brief, but productive, period in office.

9 Malcolm X (1925–65)
In 1940, Malcolm Little came to live with his sister in Boston. Here his life was significantly changed when he converted and joined the Nation of Islam while serving a burglary term in Charlestown Jail from 1946 to 1952. As Malcolm X, he became a human rights activist and Civil Rights leader before his assassination in 1965.

10 Michelle Wu (b. 1985)
In a historic election in 2021, Michelle Wu was elected mayor of Boston, making her the first person of color and woman elected to this office. In 2013, she had been elected to the office of Boston City Councilor. Wu is a graduate of Harvard University and Harvard Law School.

Michelle Wu, Boston's mayor, speaking to the public

TOP 10
LITERARY BOSTONIANS

Author Dorothy West

1. Anne Bradstreet *(c. 1612–72)*
America's first poet, Bradstreet published *The Tenth Muse, Lately Sprung Up in America* in 1650.

2. Ralph Waldo Emerson *(1803–82)*
Poet and philosopher, Emerson espoused transcendentalism as well as pioneering American literary independence.

3. Henry Wadsworth Longfellow *(1807–82)*
Longfellow is best known for epic poems such as *Hiawatha*.

4. Louisa May Alcott *(1832–88)*
Little Women sealed the literary fame of Alcott.

5. Henry James *(1843–1916)*
Master of sonorous prose, James is considered one of the creators of the psychological novel.

6. Dorothy West *(1907–98)*
African American novelist and essayist, West made sharp observations about class and race conflicts.

7. Elizabeth Bishop *(1911–79)*
A poet and a short story writer, Bishop was known for her witty and expressive verse.

8. Robert Lowell *(1917–77)*
The "confessional poetry" of Lowell went on to influence a whole generation of writers.

9. Robert Parker *(1932–2010)*
Scholar of mystery literature, Parker is known for his detective Spenser.

10. Dennis Lehane *(b. 1965)*
Novelist Dennis Lehane brings a dark, tragic vision to the working-class neighborhoods of Boston.

WATERFRONT AREAS

1 The Esplanade
M3

Provided the Charles River Basin has not frozen over, collegiate rowing crews, canoeists, small sailboats, and the occasional Coast Guard patrol all share the waters off the Esplanade. Find a bench facing the water and take in the scene.

2 Castle Island
2010 Day Blvd, South Boston

Connected to the mainland via an earthen causeway and crowned by the c. 1851 Fort Independence, Castle Island is New England's oldest continually fortified site. Aside from exploring the fort's bunkers and tunnels (in season), visitors enjoy fine panoramic views of Boston Harbor.

3 Constitution Beach
Bennington St, East Boston

Views of Downtown don't get much better than those from this tastefully revitalized beach and park area in East Boston. A clean beach, picnic areas, and lifeguards make this a favorite with families.

4 Piers Park
B5 **Marginal St, East Boston**

Piers Park offers amazing views of the downtown Boston skyline. The main pier, extending far into the harbor, is crowned with a pavillion dedicated to Donald McKay, master shipbuilder. Here he built some of the world's fastest clipper ships.

5 Long Wharf
R3

Long Wharf has been indispensable to Boston's merchant industry for over 300 years. Given the wharf's deep frontage and proximity to waterfront warehouses, the biggest ships of their day could dock here. Today, ferry services and cruise vessels depart from here, creating a spirited dock scene, and there's excellent waterside dining at a branch of the restaurant Legal Sea Foods.

6 Boston Fish Pier

This pier is a solid reminder of the city's roots in the fishing trade. Built in 1912–14, the pier was the largest and most modern facility of its kind at that time. The day's catch is still brought to the early morning market here. Sample some of it in hearty chowders and the decadent dishes served in Boston's seafood restaurants (*p68*).

7 Fort Point Channel
H5

Fort Point has lured artists to the neighborhood with affordable studio

Leafy Piers Park on Boston's waterfront

High-rise buildings overlooking Fort Point Channel

space in old warehouse buildings. Open studios in May and October offer a peek inside and a chance to bag a bargain on artwork. Today, the neighborhood houses the $300-million Federal Courthouse and trendy cafés and restaurants.

8 Rowes Wharf
🖭 R3

Framed by the colossal atrium of the Boston Harbor Hotel *(p149)*, Rowes Wharf is a popular docking spot for the high-end harbor cruise outfits and is a luxurious contrast to the city's grittier, saltier working docks. The hotel sponsors free concerts and film screenings on summer evenings.

9 Langone Park
🖭 H2

North End's Langone Park is located right on the waterfront, looking out toward Charlestown. On warm days, the neighborhood's old guard comes here to enjoy a game or two of *bocce* (bowls). Nearby, children play baseball or splash around in the outdoor pool.

10 Seaport District
🖭 H4

This bustling waterfront development encompasses the historic shipping and fishing piers east of Fort Point Channel. Today, the area is a vibrant mix of hotels, bars, and entertainment.

TOP 10
SCENIC VIEWS

1. Weeks Footbridge
🖭 B2
A prime spectator spot during the Head of the Charles Regatta *(p60)*.

2. Longfellow Bridge
🖭 M2
View the Charles River Basin on the "T" between Kendall and Charles/MGH.

3. City Experiences
🖿 cityexperiences.com
Admire the city from the water as you enjoy brunch, lunch, drinks, or dinner.

4. Charlestown Bridge
🖭 G2
This bridge offers splendid harbor and Downtown vistas.

5. John J. Moakley Courthouse Park
🖭 H4
This beautiful waterfront park has fine views of the towering Financial District.

6. Hyatt Regency Cambridge
🖭 C4 🏠 575 Memorial Dr
Enjoy skyline views across the Charles River from the Paperback Tavern bar.

7. Independence Wharf Deck
🖭 R4
The observation deck atop 470 Atlantic Ave has great views of Seaport District.

8. Dorchester Heights Monument
🖭 Q3 🏠 15 State St
The park around this commemorative spire offers broad views of the harbor.

9. Hyatt Regency Boston Harbor
🏠 101 Harborside Dr, East Boston
The Hyatt's Harborside Grill and Patio offers panoramic Boston views.

10. Bunker Hill Monument
Climb the monument *(p45)* to see the city laid out before you.

Bunker Hill Monument

BOSTON HARBOR ISLANDS

1 Georges Island

🚢 Long Wharf (mid-May–mid-Oct); bostonharborislands.org

Georges Island is the gateway to the Boston Harbor Islands National and State Park, which includes 34 islands and mainland parks. Here, visitors can hike, explore historic buildings, bird-watch, and visit the Civil War-era Fort Warren, where there's a snack bar and visitor center. See the website for information on all Boston Harbor islands.

2 Peddocks Island

Peddocks is one of Boston Harbor's largest and most diverse islands. Hiking trails circle a pond, salt marsh, and coastal forest, and pass by Fort Andrews, which was active in harbor defense from 1904 through to World War II. The island is known for the beach plums and wild roses that bloom profusely in the dunes. A visitor center and campsite make it an overnight destination.

3 Lovells Island

Known for its extensive dunes, Lovells also has an unsupervised swimming beach. Extensive hiking trails lead across the dunes and through woodlands. The remains of Fort Standish, which was built

Visitors exploring Fort Warren on Georges Island

in 1907 and was active during the Spanish American War and World War I, can also be explored.

4 Grape and Bumpkin Islands

Both these islands are a delight for naturalists – Grape for its wildflowers, raspberries, and bayberries, and Bumpkin for its wild roses and birdlife. On Bumpkin Island, hiking trails pass the ruins of a farmhouse and 19th-century children's hospital, which also housed German prisoners rescued from Boston Harbor in World War I and later polio patients, before burning down in 1945. Remains of the hospital can still be seen.

5 Deer Island

Accessed by a causeway from the mainland, part of this island was opened in 2006 for recreation and walking, and it offers dramatic views of the Boston skyline. Deer Island is also known for its impressive, state-of-the-art $3.8 billion sewage treatment plant. Distinguished by 12 gigantic egg-shaped digesters, it was key to cleaning up Boston Harbor.

6 Spectacle Island

Featuring some of the highest peaks of the harbor islands, Spectacle Island has the best Boston skyline view. The construction of a snack bar and visitor center has made it one of the most popular of all the harbor islands. Visitors can enjoy 5 miles (8 km) of trails, including the ADA Accessible Perimeter Trail, and beaches with lifeguards.

7 Gallops Island

🚫 To the public

Once the site of a popular summer resort, Gallops also served as quarters for Civil War soldiers, including the Massachusetts 54th Regiment (p28). The island has an extensive sandy beach, a picnic area, hiking paths, and historic ruins of a former quarantine and immigration station. The Massachusetts Department of Conservation and Recreation has closed the island indefinitely for a thorough environmental clean-up.

8 Little Brewster Island

🚫 To the public

Boston Light, the first US lighthouse, was constructed here in 1716 and continues to cast a light beam that reaches 27 miles (44 km). From 2003 to 2023 it was staffed by Sally Snowman, the light's 70th caretaker and its first female keeper. Check the Boston Harbor Islands website for the schedule of weekly cruises that sail past Boston Light.

9 Thompson Island

A learning center since the 1830s, Thompson is the site of an Outward Bound program serving more than 5,000 students annually. The island's diverse landscape includes rocky and sandy shores, a large salt marsh, sumac groves, and a hardwood forest. Herons, killdeer, and shorebirds abound. Ferries depart from EDIC Pier off Summer St on weekends from May to October.

10 World's End

🕸 thetrustees.org ♿

This 0.4-sq-mile (1-sq-km) peninsula overlooking Hingham Bay is a geological sibling of the harbor islands, with its two glacial drumlins, rocky beaches, ledges, cliffs, and both salt and freshwater marshes. Frederick Law Olmsted (p29) laid out the grounds for a homestead development here in the late 19th century. The homes were never built, but carriage paths, formal plantings, and hedgerows remain. World's End is operated by Trustees of Reservations and accessed by road via Hingham. There's an admission fee to the site for nonmembers.

Little Brewster Island, with its historic lighthouse

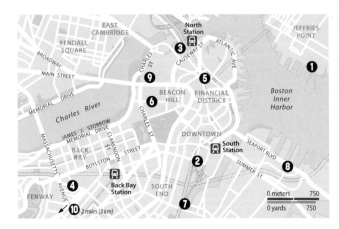

OFF THE BEATEN PATH

1 ICA Watershed
⌂ Boston Harbor Shipyard & Marina, 256 Marginal St ⏰ 10am–5pm Tue–Sun (to 9pm Thu & Fri) 🌐 icaboston.org

The summer outpost of the ICA *(p100)* mounts an innovative installation each year. A free shuttle from the ICA to the Watershed is available with a ticket purchase.

2 South Street Diner
📍 Q5 ⌂ 178 Kneeland St ⏰ 24 hrs daily 🌐 southstreetdiner.com

Built in 1947 as a lunch car for factory workers, South Street is one of the Worcester Dining Company's iconic metal car diners. Long known as the Blue Diner, it has featured in many Hollywood films and has been a late-night hangout for students, musicians, and night owls.

3 The Sports Museum
📍 P1 ⌂ TD Garden, 100 Legends Way ⏰ Noon–3:30pm daily ⏰ On event days, check website 🌐 sports museum.org 📷 📷

Spread over two floors above the TD Garden, home of the Bruins (ice hockey) and Celtics (basketball), are displays on all the city's renowned teams. The collection includes a section of the wooden seats from the original Boston Garden, where you can watch screenings of historic games.

4 Christian Science Mapparium™
📍 K6 ⌂ 210 Massachusetts Ave ⏰ 10am–5pm Mon–Sat, 11am–5pm Sun 🌐 christianscience.com/ howdoyouseetheworld 📷 📷

Accessed only by paid timed ticket, the three-story-high stained-glass

Retro South Street Diner, Boston's only all-night hangout

The stained-glass Mapparium™ globe at the Christian Science Plaza

Mapparium™ globe is viewed from the interior while standing on a glass walkway. Illuminated by LED lighting, the countries represented on the globe's surface reflect the geopolitical boundaries of the world that existed when it was built in 1935. The globe is part of an exhibit called "How Do You See the World?", which highlights humanity's achievements since 1935 in the fields of human rights, scientific breakthroughs, and exploration.

5 The New England Holocaust Memorial

🅠 Q2 🅐 Between Congress and Union sts

Six luminous glass towers soar above a black granite path to remember the atrocities undertaken by the Nazi regime. The structures represent the six main death camps and the six million Jews who died during the six years of World War II.

6 Pinckney Street

🅜 M3

This charming street, with its cobbled sidewalks, old-school street lamps, and brick row houses, has been home to numerous writers. Philosopher Henry David Thoreau lived at No. 4, Irish poet Louise Imogen Guiney at No. 16, and Louisa May Alcott (of *Little Women* fame) at Nos. 20, 43, and 81. Just imagine the kind of neighborhood book club they would have had they crossed paths.

7 Underground at Ink Block

🅖 G5 🅐 90 Traveler St
🅦 undergroundinkblock.com

Located under the South End–South Boston highway underpass, this urban park is an explosion of creativity, with annually changing, colorful murals that are both beautiful and provocative.

8 The Lawn on D

🅗 H5 🅐 420 D St 🅞 Dawn to dusk
🅦 signatureboston.com/lawn-on-d

One of Boston's most popular green spaces, the Lawn on D is located in the heart of the Seaport District and is close to the Convention and Exhibition Center. This hip outdoor space features live music, art exhibitions, lawn games, and food trucks. Check the website for upcoming events.

9 Paul S. Russell, MD Museum of Medical History and Innovation

🅝 N2 🅐 Massachusetts General Hospital, 2 North Grove St 🅞 10am–2pm Tue–Fri, 11am–4pm Sat
🅦 massgeneral.org/museum

This museum traces medical innovation with displays, artifacts, and guides. The Ether Dome, nearby, was the site of the first successful use of ether anesthetic in surgery.

10 Samuel Adams Brewery

🅐 30 Germania St
🅦 samadamsboston brewery.com

This lively tour of the Samuel Adams craft brewery takes you through the process and offers free tastings of Samuel Adams' famous beers. Note that tour tickets should be reserved in advance.

A bottle of Samuel Adams craft beer

FAMILY ATTRACTIONS

1 Children's Museum

This venerable funhouse (p101) pioneered the interactive exhibit concept now found in museums worldwide. It includes a climbing wall, a Big Dig-style construction zone, and a science playground where tracks, balls, and bubbles encourage kids to make learning fun. The museum runs a program of special events covering a range of subjects, including health, engineering, and literacy.

2 Boston Duck Tours

K6 ☐ Prudential Center, New England Aquarium, and Museum of Science ☐ Apr–Nov: 9am–dush daily ☒ bostonducktours.com ☐

Board a World War II-style amphibious vehicle that plies the Charles River as smoothly as it navigates Back Bay streets. This historic tour encompasses the entire peninsula and is conducted by informative and entertaining guides.

3 Swan Boats

☐ N4 ☐ Public Garden ☐ Mid-Apr–early Sep: from 10am daily ☒ swanboats.com ☐

If Boston were to have a mascot, it would likely sport white feathers and an arching neck. Round up the whole family and take to the Public Garden's lagoon on one of the city's swan boats (p29).

4 Museum of Science

Hands-on learning exhibits at this museum (p26), such as assembling animal skeletons

A Boston Duck Tours vehicle

or building a computer model, teach children the thrill of discovery. The Omni Theater delights with its fast-paced IMAX® projections, while the planetarium places the cosmos within reach. There are also 4D film presentations and an insect zoo.

5 New England Aquarium

The aquarium (p46) goes to great lengths to keep kids entertained through a variety of interactive displays. Children are typically transfixed by penguins hopping and waddling in their rocky enclosure, and by the clowning antics of the harbor seals.

6 Martin's Park

⚅ R5 ⚅ 64 Sleeper St
Named in honor of Martin Richard, the youngest victim of the 2013 Boston Marathon Bombing, this vibrant playground park is a welcome respite in the urban Seaport District.

7 Legoland® Discovery Center

⚅ 598 Assembly Row, Assembly Sq Mall, Somerville ⚅ From 10am daily; closing hours vary, check website ⚆ legodiscoverycenter.com ⚇
A family entertainment center clubbed with a multiplex cinema, Legoland® is a prime attraction for children aged between 3 and 10. In addition to incredible tableaux made of Lego® bricks, the center has Lego® rides, a soft play center, and a bevy of Lego® characters. The highlight for many is the chance to build and test Lego® racers.

8 Frog Pond

Boston Common's Frog Pond (p28) is a great place for families to visit year-round. As soon as temperatures dip below freezing, kids flock here for ice-skating and hot chocolate at the adjacent hut. In spring, the Common's mid-20th-century carousel, located next to the pond, starts spinning and is ready to delight riders. During Boston's oft-oppressive summer

Kermit the Frog's statue sitting on the edge of Frog Pond

days, families descend on Frog Pond for splashing and fun beneath the central fountain. Then, in fall, there's the annual Fall-o-Ween festival. Held by the pond, this free event brings Halloween thrills to the Common, with attractions including a haunted maze and a glow-in-the-dark play area, as well as arts and crafts, and live music.

9 Greenway Carousel

⚅ R1 ⚅ Rose Kennedy Greenway ⚆ rosekennedygreenway.org ⚇
Set inside the Rose Kennedy Greenway, this charming seasonal carousel features hand-carved figures of 14 local animals, including a squirrel, turtle, cod, lobster, whale, three types of butterfly, and more. It is also accessible to individuals with specific requirements.

10 Bouldering Project

⚅ 12A Tyler St, Somerville ⚅ 6am–11pm Mon–Fri, 8am–10pm Sat & Sun ⚆ bouldering project.com ⚇
Adorned with sprawling rock climbing walls and rope courses, this Somerville recreation center is perfect for teenagers burning off some pent-up energy on a rainy day. Visitors must be 14 years or over to participate and advance reservations online are recommended.

SPORTS AND OUTDOOR ACTIVITIES

A Boston Red Sox player batting at Fenway Park

2019, ultimately earning six Superbowl rings before retiring from the Patriots. To watch the team today, head an hour outside of Boston to Foxboro's Gillette Stadium (*gillettestadium.com*), or see the game from the comfort of Cask 'n Flagon (*p122*) next to Fenway Park.

4 Ice Hockey

To watch a world-class ice hockey game, head to TD Garden, base of the Boston Bruins (they share it with the Celtics). If you're visiting in February, grab tickets to the Boston Beanpot, which sees four Massachusetts universities (Harvard, Boston University, Boston College, and Northeastern) all convene to battle for hockey supremacy.

5 Sailing and Rowing

Thanks to the winding Charles River and expansive Boston Harbor, the city is a popular spot for boating. Take to the water with Classic Sail Boston (*classicsail boston.com*), which offers a variety of sailing trips in the harbor. Alternatively, time your visit for the Head of the Charles Regatta; occurring during late October, this rowing race draws participants from across the globe.

6 Hiking

In spite of its small size, the state of Massachusetts has some incredible pockets of natural beauty, with Blue Hills Reservation and Middlesex Fells serving as two just beyond Boston limits. The first is best known for its lengthy hiking trails and scenic Boston skyline views from its peak, while the latter offers idyllic walking paths along multiple reservoirs.

7 Cycling

The Greater Boston area has developed an extensive cycling scene, with bike paths lacing all the way from the western suburbs to the mouth of

1 Baseball

For well over a century, the beloved Boston Red Sox have played their home games at Fenway Park (*p119*), the oldest active stadium in Major League Baseball (don't miss the hand-turned scoreboard). Visiting sports fans are welcome to attend a regular season game from April to October, while history buffs can discover the inner workings of the park during a daily guided tour.

2 Basketball

The Celtics have called TD Garden home since 1995, and there's no better spot to dive into the history of basketball than the on-site Sports Museum (*p56*). Here, you'll learn about the invention of the sport in the Massachusetts city of Springfield. Afterward, stick around to catch a live game.

3 NFL

Tom Brady and Bill Belichek cemented themselves as New England royalty in the period from 2001 to the Charles River. While self-guided excursions are available all across the area, the Emerald Necklace (p29) is perfect for a leisurely cruise along Boston's verdant public parks system.

8 Kayaking

To see the city from a different perspective, rent a kayak and paddle down the Charles River. During the warmer months, Paddle Boston (paddleboston.com) offers a fleet of kayaks, canoes, and paddleboards to rent along with an array of guided tours.

9 Bird-watching

The biodiversity of New England is on full display at Mass Audubon's Boston Nature Center (massaudubon.org). The surrounding wetlands host a wealth of native mammals, insects, and reptiles – and you'll likely glimpse some of the resident birds, such as the black-capped chickadee and the northern cardinal.

10 Running

It's no secret that Boston has a deep affinity for running – the world-famous Boston Marathon has been a treasured tradition since 1897, after all. You can catch this spectacle in late April, but outside of the race, places like the Waterfront and Charles River Esplanade are perfect for lacing up and hitting the paved paths for a run with the locals.

Runners pounding the streets during the Boston Marathon

TOP 10 WALKS AND CYCLES

1. Pleasure Bay
A 2-mile (3-km) walk passes around this sandy bay (p134) to Castle Island, known for its historic fort, before looping back to land via a causeway.

2. Jamaica Pond
A variety of lakeside paths wind around this large body of water (p133), drawing crowds of visitors for walking, jogging, bike riding, and bird-watching.

3. Chestnut Hill Reservation
355 Chestnut Hill Ave, Brighton
There are 1.5 miles (2 km) of walking trails to enjoy along this preserve, with no shortage of fishing spots for a relaxing day on the reservoir.

4. Back Bay Fens
Take a gentle pootle by bike around this verdant Fenway park (p120) to discover gardens, skyline views, and a whole lot of curious geese.

5. Carson Beach
This sandy South Boston stretch of coastline springs to life when the weather turns warm, drawing visitors for a lengthy stroll along its shores.

6. Mount Auburn Cemetery
Spend a couple of hours strolling along the tree-lined paths of this burial ground, which is dotted with the graves of famous locals (p74).

7. Deer Island
This peninsula (p54) is threaded by a number of lengthy hiking trails, which offer striking vantage points of the Boston skyline.

8. Magazine Beach
B4 668 Memorial Dr, Cambridge
This scenic strip of sand is perfect for a long walk by the water.

9. Mary Ellen Welch Greenway
Take a walk from Jeffries Point Waterfront to Constitution Beach (p52) along this picturesque greenway.

10. Franklin Park
Home to wild deer and turkeys, Boston's largest park (p133) is criss-crossed with winding bike paths.

NIGHTS OUT

1 Symphony Hall
Renowned for its superb acoustics, this historic structure (p119) is the home of both the Boston Symphony Orchestra and Boston Pops Orchestra; the former serves up stunning performances of classical music, while the latter puts a new spin on styles like pop, jazz, and indie rock.

2 Boston's Jazz Scene
Thanks in part to the city's music schools, such as Berklee and the New England Conservatory, Boston has a booming jazz scene. To immerse yourself in the genre, swing by the Mad Monkfish (themadmonkfish.com) for sophisticated music, or visit the Beehive (p115), one of the world's best jazz venues, for a refined cocktail served in a boudoir-like, bohemian setting.

3 Live Rock
The birthplace of both Aerosmith and the Pixies, Boston has no shortage of iconic venues for rocking out in. The aptly named Paradise Rock Club (967 Commonwealth Ave) has served as a stomping ground for acts like Blondie and Red Hot Chili Peppers in years past, while the Orpheum Theatre (1 Hamilton Pl) hosts all sorts of rock groups.

4 Irish Pubs
Boston's status as a historic hub for Irish immigration has imbued the city with a massive array of Celtic-inspired pubs, with South Boston serving as its centerpiece. L Street Tavern (p136) is a particular highlight thanks to its many Irish American decorative flourishes lining the walls.

5 Comedy Shows
Boston has a talent for comedy, with renowned comics like Seth Meyers and Bill Burr both hailing from the area. Catch soon-to-be-famous, local talent at Nick's Comedy Stop (nickscomedy stop.com) or head to Laugh Boston (laughboston.com) to see big-name comics take to the stage.

6 Ghost Tours
One of the oldest cities in the US, it's no wonder that Boston is allegedly home to a fair few spooks, specters, and spirits. For a deep dive on the city's most haunted neighborhoods, Ghosts and Gravestones (ghostsandgrave stones.com) conducts a particularly hair-raising tour that highlights centuries-old cemeteries, colonial-era execution sites, and tales of local serial killers all in one fell swoop.

Rock performers at the Paradise Rock Club

The richly decorated interior of the Boch Center – Wang Theatre's Grand Lobby

7 Theater

The city isn't short on options for theater buffs, with the Boch Center – Wang Theatre (p111) and Boston Center for the Arts (p111) both hosting an array of performances, including comedy tours, dance productions, and speaker series. Musical theater fans should head to the Citizens Bank Opera House (citizensbankoperahouse.com), which stages famed Broadway shows.

8 Cocktail Bars

Bostonians love their beer, but the city is no stranger to stellar cocktails. During a cocktail crawl across the city, don't miss the North End's Bricco (bricco. com) for a masterfully crafted espresso martini. Meanwhile, the Yellow Door Taqueria (p137) excels at the art of the margarita, offering flavors like spiced peach, mango, and blueberry maple.

9 Clubs

While Boston isn't particularly known for its club scene, that doesn't mean that there aren't late-night venues to dance the night away in. Royale (p115) serves as a draw for partygoers thanks to its large dance floor and celebrity DJs, while the more intimate, LGBTQ+ friendly Club Café (p65) is ideal for busting moves beneath a disco ball.

10 Sunset Cruise

Boston's island-dotted harbor is perfect for an evening cruise, and one of the best is the Sunset Sightseeing Cruise with City Experiences (p53). Here, you can bask in the glow of twilight, watching as both the ocean and the city skyline are illuminated by golden light.

TOP 10
LOCALLY BREWED BEERS

1. Awake, Night Shift
Porter aged with coffee picks you up and puts you down.

2. Harpoon IPA, Harpoon
Ranked among the top domestic and imported India pale ales by *Beer Connoisseur Magazine*.

3. Casual Gods, Cambridge Brewing Company
A superb barrel-fermented golden wild ale with a fruity yeast character.

4. Congress Street IPA, Trillium
Tropical fruit notes and citrusy hops dominate this flagship IPA at Trillium.

5. 617 Hazy IPA, Lord Hobo
Named after the Boston telephone area code, this beer packs a punch at 6.17 percent alcohol by volume.

6. Boston Lager, Samuel Adams
The beer that put Sam back on the brewing map after a 200-year hiatus.

7. Metric Systems, Lamplighter
Only at Cambridge taproom, this lemon-tangy Gose wheat beer is a brewery signature.

8. Cherry Wheat Ale, Samuel Adams
Like a hybrid between champagne and cherry soda, this brew is available at most liquor stores.

9. UFO Hefeweizen, Harpoon
Try this unfiltered, Belgian-style brew, with fruity undertones.

10. Octoberfest, Samuel Adams
Sam's finest – available only during fall – with deep amber coloring and a warm, spicy smoothness.

Samuel Adams tankards

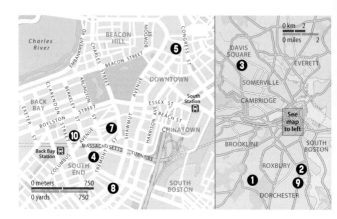

LGBTQ+ VENUES

1 Midway Café

📍 3496 Washington St, Jamaica Plain 🌐 midwaycafe.com ♿

Having offered its stage to rockabilly, punk, swing, reggae, and hip-hop acts since 1987, the Midway Café is partially responsible for Jamaica Plain's youth-driven renaissance. The club's Thursday Queeraoke Night is one of the most popular lesbian club night events in town, while other nights of the week bring in edgy music lovers from all over the city.

2 dbar

This inviting Dorchester spot (p136), with its warm wood and brass interior, has a dual personality: trendy, full-service neighborhood bistro by day, popular gay dance club at night. Love Broadway musicals? "Show Tunes Tuesdays" are a wildly popular sing-along that can get a bit rowdy late in the evening.

3 Diesel Café

📍 257 Elm St, Somerville 🌐 diesel-cafe.com

This hipster-filled coffee shop, in the heart of Somerville's bustling Davis Square, is a favorite hangout among the area's LGBTQ+ couples.

Here, they guzzle gourmet coffee, sip inventive teas, and snack on tasty treats, while soaking up the relaxed vibe and chatting the afternoon away.

4 Trophy Room

📍 M6 📍 26 Chandler St 🌐 trophyroomboston.com ♿

A part of StayPineapple hotel in the South End, this gastro bar's interior has a chic designer look. A local LGBTQ+ crowd pops in for the tasty cocktails, including the Naked Experience (a mix of bourbon, pineapple juice, and lemonade), as well as the delicious pizza and light bites that are served in the evenings. The brunch scene on Sundays can get surprisingly raucous.

5 The Alley Bar

📍 P3 📍 Pi Alley, 275 Washington St 🌐 thealleybar.com

Hosting activities like karaoke and pool tournaments, The Alley has a mellow, sociable vibe. There is an upstairs/downstairs set-up which gives the casual drinkers a space away from the theme-night partiers. The bar's menu consists of comfort American food, including chicken wings, and a range of draft and bottled beers.

Revelers enjoying a Lesbian Night Life rooftop party

6 Lesbian Night Life
W lesbiannightlife.com

This company organizes LGBTQ+ events at various venues in Boston and across New England. There are dance nights, boat cruises, and pool parties, as well as a monthly tea dance on the rooftop of Dorchester Brewing Company during the summer. Check the website for details.

7 Jacque's Cabaret
One of the oldest names on the Boston gay club scene, and discreetly tucked away behind the Theater District, Jacque's (p115) has been welcoming queer rock bands and drag queens, and their adoring fans, for many decades. It is a lively option every night of the week, with garage rock and beer fueling the pool-playing crowd.

8 Cathedral Station
N6   1222 Washington St
W cathedralstation.com

Located in the South End near Holy Cross Cathedral, this casual and spacious neighborhood sports bar is geared toward an LGBTQ+ clientele, but everyone is welcome. This venue is also the de facto home of several LGBTQ+ sports leagues.

9 Blend
1310 Dorchester Ave   W blend dorchester.com

With a tap menu heavy on local brews and fantastic pub food, Blend is a local favorite. It organizes disco nights, drag events, and screenings of RuPaul's TV show hosted by local drag legend Harlow Havoc. There's a Glitter disco on the third Friday of every month and tasty tacos every Thursday evening.

10 Club Café
M6   209 Columbus Ave
W clubcafe.com

This multifunctional South End space combines cabaret, a piano bar, a dance club, and an American bistro, drawing in a young crowd each night. Check out the video lounge, order a drink from the mirrored bar or the sleek cocktail lounge, or opt to chow down on the famous Sunday brunch. The restaurant gives classic continental fare an inspired twist.

Classy interior of Club Café

LOCAL DISHES

Boston cream pie, a Massachusetts icon

lobster boil, which is simply served alongside plenty of butter or in a broth with potatoes, corn, and other seafood.

1 Boston Cream Pie

Officially designated the state dessert of Massachusetts in 1996, the Boston cream pie unites sponge cake, custard, and a rich chocolate glaze. It's best to sample this dessert straight from its birthplace – the stately Omni Parker House (p149) – but, if you're strapped on time, an order from Flour Bakery + Café (p71) will hit the spot as well.

2 New England Clam Chowder

Few dishes represent Massachusetts as well as clam chowder, a thick stew that's particularly popular on a cold winter day. It's typically loaded with potatoes, bacon, and (of course) clams, and while Boston restaurants like Saltie Girl (p97) and Neptune Oyster (p103) have perfected the dish, diners should also swing by the Banks Fish House (p97) to sample it in flatbread form.

3 Lobster Roll

The Northeast's cold-water lobsters – sometimes called Boston lobsters – have given rise to one of New England's most iconic dishes: the lobster roll. New Englanders are embroiled in an endless battle over the superiority of hot Connecticut-style or cold Maine-style, so while you're in Boston try both versions at the Barking Crab (p103) to pick your favorite. Alternatively, try a

4 Oysters

Several Massachusetts towns are renowned for their high-quality oysters, but Boston is no slouch when it comes to shellfish either. You can find a stellar selection of East Coast oysters at venues like Eventide Fenway (p123) and the aptly named Union Oyster House (unionoysterhouse.com), while many of Boston's seafood restaurants offer $1 oyster specials throughout the year.

5 Fried clams

Whether you spring for classic strips or the New England-style "whole-bellies," no trip to Boston is complete without partaking in a round of fried clams. In Cambridge, Courthouse Seafood (p131) serves an excellent fried clam roll, while B&G Oysters (p117) is a top South End spot for sampling the dish in its purest form – straight from the shell.

6 Shepherd's Pie

This comfort food has played a major role in British and Irish cuisine for centuries, and – largely thanks to the city's Irish heritage – Boston is rife with charming pubs that specialize in the dish. Be sure to enjoy shepherd's pie to the tune of live music in Somerville at the Burren (p130), or head to Jamaica Plain spot the Haven (p136), where you can pair the dish with a high-end Scotch.

7 Pizza

Though not quite as established in cities like New York and Chicago, Boston does have its fair share of incredible pizzerias, thanks to its Italian American community. Tourists tend to flock to the North End (aka Little Italy) to get their

A chef adding swirls of chocolate to the ends of a cannoli

fix at the iconic Pizzeria Regina *(p103)*, but those willing to venture over to Cambridge to Area Four *(p131)* will be rewarded with a wide array of eclectic pies, including those topped with apple-winter squash and sherry-maple bacon.

8 Gnocchi
Piping-hot and brimming with Italian herbs and spices, gnocchi has earned worldwide acclaim as an Italian comfort food. To taste Boston's best take on this foodstuff, the North End's Mare Oyster Bar *(p103)* is the place to go; here, they serve up these little potato dumplings with a generous helping of fresh seafood, including shrimp, scallops, and calamari.

9 Doughnuts
The Greater Boston-born Dunkin' Donuts has more than 10,000 locations across the globe, and the city's prowess at doughnut-making is not fading any time soon. Blackbird Doughnuts *(blackbirddoughnuts.com)* has options ranging from classic vanilla glaze to Boston cream pie-inspired. And for top-notch vegan choices, don't miss Union Square Donuts *(p71)*.

10 Cannoli
This popular Italian sweet treat consists of a fried pastry shell with a creamy ricotta filling. Mike's Pastry *(p102)* has been a local favorite since the 1940s due to its mastery of the craft, but nearby places like Modern Pastry *(p102)* and Bova's Bakery *(p102)* have similar offerings without the hassle of waiting in a lengthy line.

TOP 10
LOBSTER BOILS

Classic lobster boil

1. The Barking Crab
This long-standing outpost *(p103)* excels at the art of a classic lobster boil.

2. Boston Sail Loft
🅡 R2 🏠 80 Atlantic Ave
Sublime seafood paired with gorgeous harbor views is offered here.

3. Yankee Lobster Company
🏠 300 Northern Ave
Jostle around the zinc bar for tasty little bites and glasses of natural wine.

4. Chart House
🅡 R3 🏠 60 Long Wharf
Come here to feast on classically prepared Maine lobster.

5. Bootleg Special
🅝 N6 🏠 400 Tremont St
Bootleg kicks up the heat with a spicy Cajun-inspired seafood boil, featuring lobster, crab legs, and jumbo prawns.

6. The Banks Fish House
The steamed lobster served here *(p97)* is packed full of corn and mashed potatoes.

7. Summer Shack
This Back Bay venue *(p97)* has perfected the classic steamed lobster.

8. James Hook & Co.
Since the 1920s, this coastal spot *(p103)* has earned citywide acclaim for its whole cooked lobsters.

9. Legal Harborside
Each one of this chain *(p103)* serves top-quality Maine lobster that's stuffed with shrimp and scallop.

10. Union Oyster House
🅠 Q2 🏠 41 Union St
This downtown venue whips up superbly cooked lobsters.

SPOTS FOR SEAFOOD

1 James Hook & Co.
A family-owned business located right on Fort Point Channel, James Hook & Co. *(p103)* is primarily a broker that supplies lobster to restaurants throughout the US. However, they also cook lobster, clams, crab, and a few types of fish on the spot. Take your order, sit on the sea wall, and chow down. This is one of the best places to eat good, reasonably priced seafood.

2 Legal Harborside
The Seaport flagship *(p103)* of the Legal Sea Foods chain has aced dockside dining. You'll find a no-frills, casual dining room, oyster bar, and a traditional fish market on level one; there's fine dining featuring beautifully prepared fish on level two; while level three offers a four-season rooftop lounge and bar, with a retractable glass roof and walls, serving ocean-fresh sushi and cocktails. All three spaces come with a stunning harbor view.

3 Neptune Oyster
Exceptionally fresh choices from the raw bar vie for attention with dishes from the expertly prepared dinner menu. Choose an old favorite,

such as clam chowder, or a more daring dish like Spanish octopus with hazelnut romesco. The simple dining room of this restaurant *(p103)* ensures that the food is the focus of attention. Reservations are not accepted so arrive early and be prepared to wait for a table – it's worth it.

4 Mare Oyster Bar
Located in Boston's historic North End, Mare *(p103)* specializes in Italian coastal cuisine. Begin with the raw bar or a trio of crudos, then savor a classic seafood pasta dish or grilled fish – or indulge yourself with a decadent lobster roll on brioche, along with a plate of fries. The spicy fish gnocchi is a must try. A few meat dishes are also available. To accompany your meal, enjoy a cocktail or glass of wine from their enticing drinks menu.

5 Courthouse Seafood
A stalwart in its Portuguese neighborhood since 1912, the Courthouse *(p131)* offers dishes prepared with the fresh catch of the day. The restaurant's menu brims with sautéed or fried squid, lightly breaded and deep-fried smelt, and

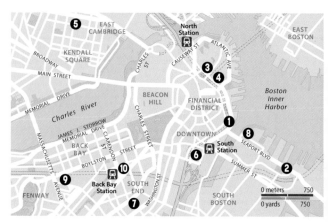

Diners arriving at the renowned Barking Crab fish shack

broiled haddock or salmon. During July to September, try the intensely flavored bluefish.

6 O Ya

Combining Japanese tradition and American invention, this elegant restaurant *(p109)* proves that good things come in small packages. Offering both sweet and savory dishes, half the menu is sushi and sashimi, and the other half is made up of meat and vegetarian options. With six chefs at work, each bite-sized portion is exquisitely executed. Ask for the *omakase* (tasting) menu and let the head chef Tim Cushman wow you with a culinary tour de force.

7 B&G Oysters

This brightly lit underground seafood spot *(p117)* is both oyster bar – there are a dozen varieties ready to be shucked at any moment – and seafood bistro.

8 Barking Crab

This colorful fish shack *(p103)* is most congenial in the summer, when diners sit outdoors at picnic tables, but there's also indoor seating with a cozy wood-burner for chillier days. Most of the local fish – cod, haddock,

tuna, halibut, clams, and crab – are so fresh that they need only the simplest preparation. There is also a good selection of wines and craft beers on offer.

9 Summer Shack

Boston celebrity chef Jasper White literally wrote the book on lobster, but he's just as adept with wood-grilled fresh fish and delicate fried shellfish. A fabulous raw bar and colorful summer fish-shack atmosphere match well with the extensive beer list. Re-creating the ambience of a beachside seafood shack in the city, this spot *(p97)* is a great place to bring kids.

10 The Banks Fish House

The seafood sister to steak-lovers' Grill 23 *(p97)*, Banks Fish House *(p97)* has a beautiful dining space, with three fireplaces, two bars, and an open kitchen, split across two levels. On any given day, the menu features oysters from a half dozen New England harbors and the latest local seasonal catch. Dine casually on chowder, pizza, or fish tacos at the bar or reserve a table to indulge in a seafood feast, complemented by a dazzling wine list.

CAFÉS

1 Thinking Cup
📍 P4 📍 165 Tremont St

A cozy place to socialize on Boston Common, Thinking Cup serves teas and Stumptown-roasted coffee. Knowledgeable baristas offer assistance with your choice of espresso drinks or pour-overs. The menu also includes tempting pastries and sandwiches.

2 Pavement Coffee
📍 J6 📍 1096 Boylston St

This local roaster offers a range of coffee roasts in everything from pour-overs to espresso. The freshly made bagels are also popular (students of the nearby Berklee College love them).

3 Caffè Vittoria
📍 Q1 📍 296 Hanover St

The jukebox at the largest of North End's Italian cafés is heavily loaded with songs recorded by Frank Sinatra, Tony Bennett, and Al Martino. The menu is long on short coffees and short drinks, including at least seven varieties of grappa, as well as Italian ices. The café accepts cash only.

4 Sorelle Bakery & Cafe
📍 H4 📍 100 Northern Ave

The Seaport branch of this local coffee and sweets emporium serves all of your regular coffee options and has a nice selection of freshly brewed teas as well. Local early risers flock here each morning for a frittata sandwich with ciabatta bread or a bowl of steel-cut oatmeal; the cranberry muffins are a hit, too.

5 Mike's Pastry
Legendary for its 20 or so flavors of fresh cannoli, Mike's Pastry (p102) is one of Boston's most loved bakeries. Here is a café where all sorts of baked goodies are available, including cupcakes, biscotti, brownies, cakes, pies, cookies, and specialty items – along with gourmet brews. The lines outside Mike's can be long, especially on weekends, but they do tend to move quickly.

6 Sonsie
📍 J6 📍 327 Newbury St

Although continental breakfast is served, Sonsie doesn't really get going until lunchtime. By dusk, it is full of folks who just stopped in for a post-work drink and ended up making an evening of it. The food – pizza, pasta, and fusion-tinged entrées – deserves more attention than most café-goers give it.

7 Tatte Bakery & Café
📍 B1 📍 1288 Massachusetts Ave, Cambridge

Featuring an artfully curated menu by master pastry chef Tzurit Or, Tatte's

Ordering breakfast at Sorelle Bakery & Cafe

A selection of baked goods at Tatte Bakery & Café

Harvard Square branch has striking decor with an open kitchen and bakery on the first floor, and a coffee bar on the second floor. Hipsters, Harvard staff and students, and locals flock here to get their fix of caffeine and heavenly pastries, tarts, cookies, as well as quiches.

8 1369 Coffee House
A community-based café, 1369 Coffee House has a definite neighborly atmosphere. The original Inman Square branch (p129) has a more interesting cross section of characters but the Central Square outpost has sidewalk seating. Both branches serve a wide selection of caffeine drinks, as well as cakes, pastries, cookies, bagels, and sandwiches.

9 Dado Tea
This eco-friendly shop (p129) serves a choice of blends, alongside organic wraps, sandwiches, and salads as well as white, black, and green teas. There's a decent selection of gluten-free and vegan options, too.

10 Phinista Cafe
🇶 D5 🇶 96 Peterborough St
This French–Vietnamese café brews *phin* coffee in all its dizzying variations. Think coffee mixed with egg yolk and condensed milk, and a vegan latte made with condensed coconut milk. The house favorite tea is *oolong*, often served with steamed milk. Star anise and cloves flavor the popular "Milk n' Thai" tea.

TOP 10
COMFORT FOOD

1. L. A. Burdick Chocolatiers
🇶 B1 🇶 52D Brattle St, Cambridge
Burdick's rich hot chocolate is one of Boston's most popular winter treats.

2. Swissbäkers
🇶 A3 🇶 168 Western Ave
This modern bakery serves pretzels, baguettes, sandwiches, and cookies.

3. Union Square Donuts
🇶 20 Bow St, Somerville
Classic doughnut flavors and surprising seasonal specialties are offered here.

4. La Sultana Bakery
🇶 40 Maverick Sq, East Boston
Empanadas and other Colombian delicacies are served at this bakery.

5. Flour Bakery + Café
🇶 F6 🇶 1595 Washington St
This chain excels at breakfast pastries, lunchtime sandwiches, and cookies.

6. FoMu
🇶 F6 🇶 655 Tremont St
A great spot for excellent vegan cookies and frappes.

7. Lizzy's Ice Cream
🇶 B1 🇶 29 Church St, Cambridge
The ice cream offered here has toppings such as chopped candy bars.

8. Sofra Bakery & Cafe
🇶 1 Belmont St, Cambridge
Try a *dukkah* (an Egyptian condiment) macaroon at this bakery.

9. Christina's Homemade Ice Cream
🇶 D2 🇶 1255 Cambridge St, Cambridge
Exciting flavors of ice cream are served with fresh fruits and spices.

10. Beacon Hill Chocolates
🇶 M3 🇶 91 Charles St
Sweet shop selling artisan chocolates from around the globe.

Beacon Hill Chocolates

ESSENTIAL SHOPPING EXPERIENCES

Browsing the shelves inside Harvard Book Store in Harvard Square

1 Harvard Square Bookstores
B1

Harvard Square's bookstores are some of the country's most distinguished. The Harvard Coop (*1400 Massachusetts Ave*) carries 170,000-plus titles, while rival Harvard Book Store (*1256 Massachusetts Ave*) stocks countless new and used books and hosts readings. Nearby Grolier Poetry Bookshop (*6 Plympton St*) is verse central, while the Million Year Picnic (*99 Mt Auburn St*) has been a top spot for comic books since the 1970s.

2 Boston Public Market
Q2 **100 Hanover St**

This public market features around 30 farmers, fishers, and other small food producers. The many food vendors make it a good breakfast or lunch option. A demo kitchen hosts various activities.

3 Garment District
D2 **200 Broadway, Cambridge**

The vintage clothing and bargain-priced trends of the Garment District are every Boston hipster's dream. Fancy-dress costumes are found on the first floor, but you can also find retro goods, office wear, and even clothing sold by the pound.

4 Faneuil Hall Marketplace
With its millions of visitors each year, Faneuil Hall Marketplace (*p105*) would not be found on any best-kept secret list. Its central location, colonial history, and plethora of food stalls in Quincy Market mean that it offers a unique retail experience. Shoppers can choose from name-brand stores such as Kate Spade or the more unusual offerings from New England artisans.

5 Copley Place
L6 **100 Huntington Ave**

This was among the country's first upscale urban shopping malls. It counts high-end stores such as Louis Vuitton, Tiffany, Neiman Marcus, and Coach as its tenants. Footwear addicts are fond of Stuart Weitzman and Jimmy Choo boutiques.

6 Red Sox Team Store
D5 **19 Jersey St**

With World Series titles dating back to 1903 and the oldest ballpark in professional baseball, the Boston Red Sox engender a fan loyalty matched by few other teams. This memorabilia shop, across the street from Fenway Park (*p119*), sells every

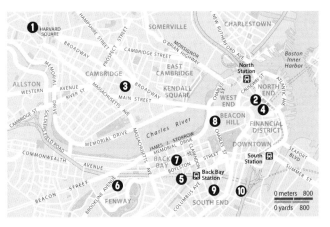

permutation of hat, jersey, and T-shirt imaginable, as well as signed bats, balls, and gloves, and baseball cards for hardcore collectors.

7 Newbury Street

Try as it might, Back Bay's most famous street cannot escape its regional reputation as the city's Beverly Hills Rodeo Drive. True, both offer stupendous people-watching, sophisticated shopping, chic dining, and prestigious galleries. Yet, with its 19th-century charm and convenient subway stops, Newbury Street (p34) outclasses its built-yesterday Left Coast counterpart by far.

8 Charles Street
🗺 M3

This charming street is studded with antiques dealers (p88), specialty grocers, and modern houseware boutiques. After dark, wrought-iron lamps illuminate the sidewalks and sleek bistros buzz with excitement.

9 Artists' Open Studios
🖥 useaboston.com

Boston's visual artists open their studios, which are mostly found in converted warehouses, to the public on selected spring and fall weekends. One of the most popular is the South End Open Studio event. Start at the Boston Center for the Arts (p111), where you can pick up a map, before exploring the many studios nearby.

10 SoWa Open Market
🗺 G6 🏠 500 Harrison Ave

Expect a wide range of clothing, jewelry, and art at Boston's art and indie design market, held every Sunday from May to October in the South End. Hungry? Check out fresh local produce at the farmers' market or take your pick from the many food trucks.

Newbury Street, the main shopping street for fashion in town

BOSTON FOR FREE

USS *Constitution*, moored at Charlestown Navy Yard

1 Charlestown Navy Yard
Home to the Revolutionary War-era frigate USS *Constitution*, the Charlestown Navy Yard (*p44*) is one of the oldest shipbuilding facilities in the country. Also here is the 1943 destroyer USS *Cassin Young*. Both admission to the yard and the ranger-led tours of the ships are free.

2 Hatch Shell
🚇 M3 🚌 47 David G. Mugar Way
🌐 hatchshell.com
Free family movie nights are held on Fridays from late June through August at the Hatch Shell, located on the banks of the Charles River. This spot also hosts free concerts throughout the summer, including Boston Pops' Fourth of July concert.

3 Mount Auburn Cemetery
🏠 580 Mt Auburn St, Cambridge
🌐 mountauburn.org
A great place to take a walk in the city is Mount Auburn Cemetery, which serves as a park, botanical garden, and arboretum, as well as the final resting place of luminaries ranging from poet Henry Wadsworth Longfellow to inventor Buckminster Fuller. The beautiful grounds feature 3 miles (5 km) of walking trails and quiet roadways.

4 Black Heritage Trail
In the 19th century, Boston's thriving Black community was a driving force in the fight to end slavery and, in the 20th century, they strove to achieve equality. A free National Park Service tour of the Black Heritage Trail (*p86*) visits a range of historic homes, schools, and businesses that tell the story of Boston's early African American citizens. Included are visits to the first public school for Black people in America and the 1806 African Meeting House.

5 Freedom Trail
Walking the self-guided Freedom Trail (*p22*) is one of the most popular activities for visitors in Boston. Touring the trail is free, as are entering all but 4 of the 16 sites and attractions along the way. Allow at least half a day for this stroll through history. For those tight on time, consider a more condensed version and visit the Old Granary Burying Ground and King's Chapel, the Old South Meeting House, the Old State House, and Faneuil Hall.

6 Harvard Square
🚇 B1 🌐 harvardsquare.com
One of Boston's liveliest public spaces is also a great place for people-watching. There are often buskers performing, and it hosts a regular schedule of events including outdoor musical and theater performances. In September, thousands of locals come to take part in the free, one-night RiverSing to celebrate the fall equinox.

The grand red-brick Georgian facade of Boston's Faneuil Hall

7 Shakespeare on Boston Common

☑ N4 ☑ commshakes.org

The Commonwealth Shakespeare Company performs one of the Bard's plays free-of-charge on Boston Common each July and August. Perfomances may be preceded by free musical concerts.

8 Boston Harborwalk

☑ bostonharbornow.org

Connecting public parks, historic sites, as well as points of interest from East Boston to Dorchester, Harborwalk is an ideal place for cycling or walking. The 43-miles (69-km) route connects the Neponset River to Belle Isle Marsh.

9 Fort Independence

Fort Independence on Castle Island (p52), at the entrance to Boston's inner harbor, was a cutting-edge military defense system when it was begun in 1834. Free tours are available in summer. Be sure to stop at Sullivan's legendary hot-dog stand, which is found nearby.

10 Free Guided Tours

There are many free guided and self-guided tours available around Boston. Three of the most popular take in the Freedom Trail (p22), Faneuil Hall (p105), and the Boston Public Library (p91). Other options include tours of Harvard Yard (p30) and the Massachusetts State House (p85).

TOP 10 BUDGET TIPS

Jazz performers at Jordan Hall

1. Music Schools
Berklee Performance Center (p93) offers low-cost and free concerts. The New England Conservatory holds free performances at Jordan Hall (p120).

2. CityPass
☑ citypass.com
A CityPass ($67) gives discounted access to four top sights.

3. Go Boston Card
☑ gocity.com
Save up to 55 percent on entry to a wide range of sights with this card.

4. Public Transit Passes
MBTA passes allow unlimited travel on subways, buses, and ferries (p141).

5. Museum Admission
Some museums, such as the Harvard Art Museums, offer free or discounted admission at certain times.

6. Special Discounts
Student and senior citizen discounts are often available with identification.

7. College Galleries
College and university art galleries offer some of the city's most provocative exhibitions, often for free.

8. Boston Symphony Savings
Reduced-price tickets for people under age 40 and limited $10 rush seats are available at Symphony Hall (p119).

9. Theater Deals
☑ huntingtontheatre.org
The Huntington Theatre has $30 tickets for under-35s; plus a limited number of $25 tickets for all ages at every show.

10. Bargain Tickets
☑ artsboston.org
Check the website for discounted tickets to many performances.

FESTIVALS AND EVENTS

1 Lunar New Year
Jan/Feb
Chinatown (p110) buzzes with the pageantry of the Lunar New Year. Streets are transformed into patchworks of color, while sidewalk vendors peddle steamed buns, soups, and other Chinese delights. Don't miss the annual parade, held the Saturday following the Lunar New Year.

2 St. Patrick's Day
Mid-Mar
Boston's immense Irish American population explains why few, if any, American cities can match its Irish pride. Come Paddy's Day, pubs host live Irish bands and raucous crowds as the Guinness and the Shamrock-green ale flow freely. The weekend South Boston Parade, with its famous drum corps, starts off from Broadway "T" station.

3 Dine Out Boston
Mar & Aug ⓦmeetboston.com/dine-out-boston
For two weeks in March and August, about 100 restaurants in Boston, Cambridge, and neighboring suburbs offer bargain, fixed-price lunch and dinner menus. Locals make the most of the opportunity to sample new places, so it is wise to make reservations.

4 Lilac Sunday
2nd Sun in May ⓦarboretum.harvard.edu
While the Arnold Arboretum (p133) includes several thousand species of flora, one plant deserves particular celebration: the lilac. When the 400 lilac plants are at their fragrant, color-washed peak, garden enthusiasts arrive for picnics, music, and walking tours of the collections.

5 Boston Calling
Late May ⓦbostoncalling.com
National headliners and new, up-and-coming acts perform live, with nonstop music for three days at the Harvard Athletic Complex. It's a family-friendly festival, with four stages and a good variety of high-energy performers and musical styles. In recent years, Boston Calling has featured the likes of the Foo Fighters, Rage Against the Machine, HAIM, and Run the Jewels.

6 Cambridge Arts River Festival
Early Jun ⓦcambridgema.gov/arts/Programs/riverfestival
On a Saturday in early June, the banks of the Charles River in Cambridge host a celebration of the city's lively and diverse population. Musicians and dancers perform and artists sell their wares. Food vendors serve a variety of cuisines.

7 Fourth of July
Jul 4
Given Boston's crucial role in securing independence for the original 13 colonies, Independence Day holds a certain importance here. With

Fireworks lighting up the sky during Boston's Fourth of July celebrations

parties, barbecues, a concert, and fireworks display over the Charles River banks, the city throws a spectacular birthday party.

8 Feast of St. Anthony
Last weekend in Aug

The Feast of St. Anthony caps an entire summer of feast holidays in the North End (p98). From noon to well into the night, Hanover Street bulges with revelers, a procession, and food vendors giving a vibrant display of the area's Italian spirit.

9 Boston Book Festival
Late Oct 🕸 bostonbookfest.org

At the end of October, book lovers gather in Copley Square for this annual celebration of the written word. The packed program includes readings, book signings, lively literary discussions, author talks, and children's storytime.

10 First Night
Dec 31

Despite the possibility of staggeringly cold weather, the New Year's Eve festivities remain among the most highly anticipated events of Boston's year. Free and open to all, the events are usually held around Copley Square and Back Bay. They include a parade, beautifully lit ice sculptures, light displays, and family-friendly fireworks at 7pm on the Common.

Visitors at Arnold Arboretum for the Lilac Sunday festival

TOP 10 NEIGHBORHOOD EVENTS

1. Roxbury International Film Festival
Late Jun 🕸 roxfilmfest.com
This lauded annual festival highlights independent films by people of color from across the globe.

2. Taste of Eastie
Jul
Discover East Boston's diverse dining scene at this charity event.

3. Revere Beach Sand Sculpting Festival
Mid-Jul 🕸 internationalsandsculptingfestival.com
Towering, elaborate sand sculptures take center stage at this long-running beachside event.

4. Fisherman's Feast
Mid-Aug 🕸 fishermansfeast.com
Since 1910 this storied North End event has served up top-tier seafood.

5. Cambridge Carnival
Early Sep 🕸 cambridgecarnival.org
Cambridge's Caribbean and African heritage is celebrated with a carnival.

6. What the Fluff?
Late Sep 🕸 flufffestival.com
A quirky event in honor of Somerville's favorite confectionery treat, Marshmallow Fluff.

7. Taste of the Fenway
Late Sep 🕸 tasteofthefenway.org
Enjoy live music and flavorful local fare a few steps from Fenway Park.

8. South Boston Street Fest
Late Sep 🕸 tasteofthefenway.org
This family-focused festival brings locals in droves to peruse more than 100 different food vendors.

9. Newton Harvest Fair
Mid-Oct 🕸 newtonma.gov
Carnival rides and pumpkin decorating stations abound at this suburban annual marketplace.

10. Jamaica Pond Lantern Parade
Late Oct
In October, thousands of Bostonians congregate along Jamaica Pond with brightly decorated homemade lamps.

DAY TRIPS: HISTORIC NEW ENGLAND

1 Lexington
🏛 Massachusetts 🚩 1875 Massachusetts Ave; lexington chamber.org

Lexington Green marks the first encounter of occupying British soldiers with organized resistance from American troops. This military band took shelter in Buckman Tavern the night before the battle. A statue memorializing this struggle stands on Lexington Battle Green. The battle is reenacted each year in mid-April.

2 Concord
🏛 Massachusetts 🚩 58 Main St; visitconcord.org

Rebels put the Redcoats to rout at North Bridge, Concord's main revolutionary battle site. The town was also the hub of American literature in the mid-19th century, and visitors can tour the homes of authors Ralph Waldo Emerson, Nathaniel Hawthorne, and Louisa May Alcott. Henry David Thoreau's woodland haunts at Walden Pond now feature hiking trails and a swimming beach.

3 New Bedford
🏛 Massachusetts 🚩 33 William St; destinationnewbedford.org

During the 19th century, New Bedford became an important port for the prosperous whaling industry. The National Historic District preserves many fine buildings of the era, and the Whaling Museum gives accounts of the enterprise.

4 Plymouth
🏛 Massachusetts 🚩 130 Water St; seeplymouth.com

The first English settlement in New England, Plymouth is home to Plimoth Patuxet Museums, which re-creates the lives of the area's Indigenous people and earliest English settlers. Explore *Mayflower II*, a replica of the ship that brought the Pilgrims to the Americas. On Thanksgiving, the town celebrates with a parade in Pilgrim dress, while many Indigenous protesters observe a National Day of Mourning.

5 Salem
🏛 Massachusetts 🚩 245 Derby St; salem.org

Known for its infamous witch trials, Salem has many other, less sensational claims to fame. Founded in 1626, it grew to become one of New England's busiest ports. Present-day Salem is a bustling town that celebrates its rich artistic and architectural heritage. Attractions include walking tours that recount the city's China Trade days (c. 1780–1880),

Alfresco dining on vibrant Atwells Avenue, Providence

and the Peabody Essex Museum – a leading interpreter of creative expressions from several cultures.

6 Providence

⌂ Rhode Island ℹ 1 Sabin St; goprovidence.com

Providence is a great walking city. Stroll Benefit Street's "mile of history" to see an impressive group of Colonial- and Federal-style houses, or visit Waterplace Park with its pretty walkways along the Providence River. Atwells Avenue on Federal Hill is Providence's Little Italy, bustling with restaurants and cafés.

7 Lowell

⌂ Massachusetts ℹ 246 Market St; nps.gov/lowe

Lowell was the cradle of the US's Industrial Revolution, where entrepreneurs dug power canals and built America's first textile mills on the Merrimack River. The sites within the National Historical Park tell parallel stories of a wrenching transformation from an agricultural to industrial lifestyle. The deafening clatter of the water-powered looms operating in the Boott Cotton Mills Museum gives a real sense of what it was like to work here.

8 Old Sturbridge Village

⌂ Massachusetts ℹ 1 Sturbridge Village Rd; osv.org

At the heart of this large living-history museum are about 40 historic buildings that have been restored and re-located from all over New England. Interpreters in period costumes go about their daily activities in a typical

A costumed person at Old Sturbridge Village

1830s village. A blacksmith works the forge, farmers tend their crops, and millers work the gristmill. Inside buildings are re-created period settings, antiques, and craft demonstrations.

9 Portsmouth

⌂ New Hampshire ℹ 500 Market St; goportsmouthnh.com

When settlers established a colony here in 1623, they called it Strawbery Banke in honor of the berries blanketing the banks of the Piscataqua River. The historic houses on Marcy Street document three centuries of city life from earliest settlement through to 20th-century immigration. Picturesque shops, pubs, and restaurants surround Market Square and line the waterfront, and the surrounding streets house fine examples of Federal architecture.

10 Newport

⌂ Rhode Island ℹ 21 Long Wharf Mall; discovernewport.org

Newport has been a playground for the rich since the late 1860s. Many of the elaborate "cottages" built by 19th-century industrialists are open for tours, including Breakers on Ochre Point Avenue. For natural beauty, hike the 3.6-mile (5.5-km) Cliff Walk overlooking Narragansett Bay and Easton's Beach.

DAY TRIPS: THE BEACH

2 Upper Cape Cod
Routes 3, 6, & 28

The Upper Cape is tranquil and lowkey. Visitors can watch the boats glide through Cape Cod Canal or take the Shining Sea bikeway from Falmouth village to Woods Hole. If it's beaches you seek, Sandwich's Sandy Neck has dunes and excellent bird-watching, but Falmouth's Surf Drive is best for swimmers and Old Silver Beach is great for sunset views.

3 Mid Cape Cod
Routes 3, 6, & 28

The Mid Cape tends to be congested, especially in the town of Hyannis. But the north shore can be peaceful, with amazing wildlife and stunning views, especially from Gray's Beach in Yarmouth. Warmer water and sandy strands line the south side of Mid Cape, with especially good swimming in Harwich and Dennisport. There's also excellent canoeing and kayaking on the Bass River.

1 Cape Ann
Routes I-95 & 127 ℹ️ **Stage Fort Park, Hough Ave, Gloucester; (978) 281-8865**

Lying 30 miles (48 km) north of Boston, the granite jaw of Cape Ann juts defiantly into the Atlantic – a rugged landscape of precipitous cliffs and deeply cleft harbors. In Gloucester, a waterfront statue and plaque memorialize the 10,000 local fishers who have perished at sea since 1623, and the Cape Ann Museum displays maritime paintings. The picturesque harborfront of Rockport is an artists' enclave and is lined with galleries.

4 Nantucket Island
Routes 3 & 6 to Hyannis, then ferry ℹ️ **25 Federal St, Nantucket; nantucketchamber.org**

The Whaling Museum in Nantucket tells the tale of the Quaker whalers who made the island prosperous in the 19th century. Today, this spot is home to luxury yachts and beach

Beachgoers enjoying the sunset at Gloucester's beach, Cape Ann

Houses and boats lining Nantucket Island's harbor

houses. Activities on the island include kayaking, casting for striped bass from Surfside Beach, or cycling to the village of Sconset with its rose-covered clifftop cottages.

5 Outer Cape Cod
Routes 3 & 6 ⓦ nps.gov/caco

With its stunning dunescapes and seemingly endless expanses of white sand it's no surprise that you'll find some of the area's best beaches here. The 40-mile (64-km) National Seashore offers great surfing at Coast Guard and Nauset Light, and the beaches of Marconi, Head of the Meadow, and Race Point all have dramatic dunes and great ocean swimming. The artist colonies of Wellfleet and Truro are worth a visit, as is Provincetown, a fishing village turned LGBTQ+ resort.

6 Martha's Vineyard
Routes 3 & 28 to Woods Hole, then ferry 🚘 24 Beach St, Vineyard Haven; mvy.com

From Vineyard Haven it's a short drive to Oak Bluffs, with its gingerbread cottages and historic carousel. Venture south to Edgartown and the 19th-century homes of rich whaling captains. Nearby, the 3-mile (5-km) Katama Beach is a magnet for sun worshipers. Southwest on the island is Menemsha, a picturesque fishing village, and Aquinnah's Gay Head Cliffs, which offer dramatic hiking routes.

7 Ipswich
Routes 95, 128, & 133, or 1A 🚘 36 South Main St; historicipswich.org

Crane Beach in Ipswich is one of New England's most scenic, with over 4 miles (6.5 km) of white sand, warm water, and outstanding bird-watching. Also on the Crane Estate, you can visit Castle Hill mansion and its lovely Italianate gardens.

8 Newburyport
Routes I-95 & 1 🚘 25 Water St; (978) 462-8681

In the 19th century, Newburyport was a prosperous seaport. The grand three-story mansions along High Street present a virtual case study in Federal architecture, while boutiques and antiques shops line downtown Merrimac, Water, and State streets. The Parker River National Wildlife Refuge on the adjacent Plum Island is one of the US's top bird-watching sanctuaries, with sandpipers, egrets, and piping plovers among its many residents and visitors.

9 Revere Beach
Routes 1 & 1A

Established in 1896, Revere Beach was the first public beach in the US. Thanks to a centennial restoration, it's also one of the best, with nearly 3 miles (4.5 km) of clean white sand and clear blue water.

10 Hampton & Rye Beaches
Routes I-95, NH 101, & 1A 🚘 160 Ocean Blvd, Hampton Beach; hamptonbeach.org

The New Hampshire coast just south of Portsmouth has extensive sandy beaches. Wallis Sands State Park is ideal for swimming but the best of the rocky overlooks is Rye's Ragged Neck Point picnic area. Odiorne Point State Park in Rye is another good picnic spot and has walking and biking trails. Hampton Beach is busiest during hot summer months, when vacationers come to enjoy the miles of golden beaches, including a designated area for surfers.

AREA BY AREA

Historic Beacon Hill

BEACON HILL

With its elegant, 19th-century row houses, friendly grocers, pricey antiques shops, and hidden gardens, Beacon Hill screams "old money" like no other area in Boston. The most exclusive block in the district is the genteel Louisburg Square, which was modeled after London's Georgian residential squares. Throughout the 19th century and well into the 20th, the charming Beacon Hill was a veritable checker-board of communities – segregated though they were.

Little of Beacon Hill's diversity has survived its inevitable gentrification, but visitors to the city can still experience the neighborhood's myriad pasts inside its opulent mansions and humble schoolhouses, and along its enchanting cobblestone streets. Beacon Hill touches on the more democratic open spaces of Boston Common and the Public Garden, and is home to the Black Heritage Trail. At the foot of this historic hill is Boston's dynamic Theater District, where grandiose playhouses perform sell-out shows.

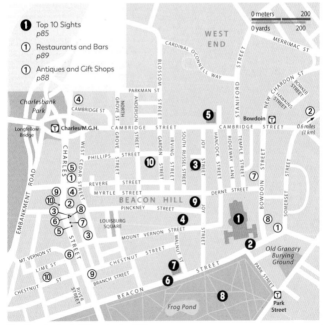

For places to stay in this area, see p148

Massachusetts State House illuminated at dusk

1 Massachusetts State House

🗺 P3 📍 24 Beacon St ⏰ For tours only Mon–Fri; reservations recommended 🌐 malegislature.gov ♿

Curious eccentricities such as a colonial-era codfish, a stained-glass image of an Indigenous American in a grass skirt, and a 23-carat gold dome crowned with a pine cone distinguish Beacon Hill's most prestigious address *(p25)*.

2 Freedom Trail

The Freedom Trail *(p22)* was established in the 1950s to provide visitors with a connect-the-dots guide to Boston's sights. It runs from Beacon Hill through Downtown, into the North End, and across the Charles River to Charlestown, which is the site of the famous warship USS *Constitution* and the Bunker Hill Monument.

3 Museum of African American History

🗺 N2 📍 46 Joy St ⏰ 10am–4pm Tue–Sun 🌐 maah.org ♿

Based in the African Meeting House (the oldest extant Black church in the US) and the adjoining Abiel Smith School (the first publicly funded grammar school for African American children in the country), the Museum of African American History (MAAH) offers a look into the daily life of free, pre-Civil War African Americans. The meeting house was a political and religious center for Boston's African American community and it was here that abolitionists such as Frederick Douglass and William Lloyd Garrison delivered antislavery addresses in the mid-19th century. The museum has successfully preserved their legacy and that of countless others through its wide and fascinating range of workshops, exhibitions, and special events.

4 Nichols House Museum

🗺 N3 📍 55 Mount Vernon St ⏰ Apr–Oct: Tue–Sun; Nov–Mar: Thu–Sun 🌐 nicholshousemuseum.org ♿

An 1804 Charles Bulfinch design, this house is one of the earliest examples of residential architecture on Beacon Hill. Rose Nichols, the house's principal occupant, bequeathed her home to the city as a museum. A pioneering force for women in the arts and sciences, Nichols gained fame through her writings on landscape architecture and her philanthropy. Tours take place on Wednesdays to Sundays at 10am, 11am and noon.

5 Harrison Gray Otis House

N2 141 Cambridge St Jun–Oct: 11am–4pm Fri–Sun historicnew england.org

One of the principal developers of Beacon Hill, Harrison Gray Otis, served in the Massachusetts legislature and gained a reputation for living the high life in this 1796 Bulfinch-designed mansion. Like a post-revolutionary Gatsby, Otis ensured his parties were the social events of the year. After falling into disrepair, the property was acquired in 1916 by the historical preservation society and has been restored to its original grandeur.

6 Beacon Street

N3

Located in the blocks between Somerset and Brimmer streets, Beacon Street features the National Historic Landmark Boston Athenaeum, one of the oldest independent libraries in the country and containing a collection of over 600,000 titles. Tours take place at the library on Mondays and Wednesdays to Saturdays. Also here are the Massachusetts State House (p85), Parkman House, and the Third Harrison Gray Otis House, at 45 Beacon St, considered architect Charles Bulfinch's finest Federal-style house. The facade of the former Bull and Finch Pub is famed as the exterior of the bar in the TV show *Cheers*.

7 Parkman House

N3 33 Beacon St
To the public

George Parkman – once a prominent physician at Harvard Medical School – lived here during the mid-19th century. In 1849, in one of the most sensationalized murder cases in US history, Parkman was killed over a financial dispute. Both the crime and its aftermath were grisly – the ensuing trial saw the inclusion of dental records as evidence for the first time, as Parkman had been partially cremated. The house is now a city-owned meeting center.

8 Boston Common

The oldest city park (p28) in the country, the Common is a

BLACK HERITAGE TRAIL

This trail takes visitors past the homes and businesses of some of Boston's most influential Black Americans, who played an indispensable role in the city's development. Maps for self-guided tours are available at the Museum of African American History. Free guided tours are led by National Park Service rangers in summer; check the website (www.nps.gov/boaf).

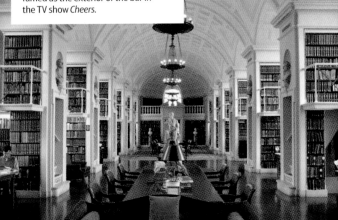

Ice-skaters on Frog Pond in Boston Common

popular gathering place for outdoor concerts, public protests, picnics in summer and, in the winter, ice-skating on Frog Pond.

9 George Middleton House
🚇 N3 📍5–7 Pinckney St
🚪 To the public

The oldest remaining private residence on Beacon Hill built by African Americans is a highlight of the Black Heritage Trail. George Middleton, a Revolutionary War veteran, commissioned the house's construction soon after the war. Legend has it that he commanded an all-Black company dubbed the "Bucks of America."

10 Boston's Center for Jewish Culture
🚇 N2 📍13–18 Phillips St 🕐 Hours vary, check website 🌐 vilnashul.org 🚪

The Vilna Shul testifies to the area's former vibrancy as Boston's first predominantly Jewish quarter. The congregation was founded in 1903 by immigrants who came from Vilna, Lithuania. The Vilna is Boston's last surviving immigrant synagogue, and today it is a center of Jewish culture with programs and exhibits. Monthly tours of the Vilna and the surrounding neighborhood are offered; book online.

Boston Athenaeum library on Beacon Street

BEACON HILL BY DAY

Morning

Take the "T" to the Charles Street/ Massachusetts General Hospital stop and exit onto **Charles Street** (p71). Enjoy a breakfast of pastries and croissants at **Tatte Bakery** (p70), then continue along Charles Street and turn right onto Beacon Street for a glimpse of the former **Bull and Finch Pub** (84 Beacon St).

Continue up Beacon to the **Massachusetts State House** (p85) for a free 45-minute weekday tour. Afterward, cross the road to the **Shaw Memorial** (p28), from where national park ranger-led **Black Heritage Trail** tours depart. The trail provides an excellent survey of the area's architectural styles as well as its Black culture sites, and concludes at the **Museum of African American History** (p85).

Afternoon

Walk back down the hill to Charles Street for a fortifying late lunch. Weather permitting, stock up on fresh fruit, a crusty baguette, and a sampling of imported cheeses at the charming **Savenor's Market** (160 Charles St) and have a picnic on **Boston Common**. Or, for diner-style fare, try sandwiches and bowls at the **Paramount** (p89). After lunch, peruse the classy paper goods at **Rugg Road** (105 Charles St) and browse Charles Street's antique shops (p88). Round the day off with a pint at **The Sevens Ale House** (p89).

Antiques and Gift Shops

A window display at Fabled Antiques on Charles Street

1. Paws on Charles
M3 **123 Charles St**
Given the ubiquity of toy dog breeds on Beacon Hill, this pet-oriented shop should come as no surprise. Expect to find tasty treats and stylish collars for your canine friend.

2. Gus & Ruby Letterpress
M3 **99 Charles St**
Gus & Ruby Letterpress is a design and print studio, offering to design formal invitations and custom stationery along with elegant paper goods, like high-end notebooks and cards.

3. Beacon Hill Chocolates
M3 **91 Charles St**
Handmade boxes of artisan chocolates, decorated with vintage Boston scenes, make ideal gifts. Don't miss the signature swirl of Caramel Sushi.

4. Rugg Road Paper Company
M3 **105 Charles St**
Rugg Road Paper Company is a treasure trove for all stationery lovers. Reflecting elegant style and sophistication, this company offers novelty items such as handmade paper, cards, gift items, and personalized stationery.

5. Boston Antiques and Lampshades
M3 **119 Charles St**
Twelve dealers operate in this space filled with treasures including Asian antiques, sculptures, estate jewelry, tableware, paintings, and much more.

6. Blackstone's of Beacon Hill
M3 **46 Charles St**
This is the place to go for unique Boston-themed gifts such as *Make Way for Ducklings (p29)* pillows and ornaments, as well as high-quality Fenway Park mugs.

7. Elegant Findings
M3 **89 Charles St** **Sun–Wed**
An intimate shop specializing in museum-quality, hand-painted 19th-century porcelain from all over Europe. You'll also find marble statuary, exquisite linens, and fine period furniture here.

8. Fabled Antiques
M3 **93 Charles St**
A refreshing emphasis on affordability and function is placed at this cozy spot. Everything from mahogany four-poster beds to belle époque opera glasses is on display.

9. The Blessing Barn
M3 **122 Charles St**
This cozy shop has a wealth of vintage paintings and trinkets. A portion of their proceeds helps fund the Room in the City project, which offers temporary stays to people who are receiving medical care in the city.

10. Helen's Leather
M3 **110 Charles St** **Tue**
While many Beacon Hill shops evoke the city's elite past, Helen's flies the flag for casual western womenswear. The chic locals swear by it for smart and warm winter boots.

Restaurants and Bars

1. Mooo
P3 **15 Beacon St** **mooo restaurant.com · $$$**
Mooo specializes in extraordinary beef and classic accompaniments at expense-account prices. The wine list includes many stellar names.

2. City Winery
Q1 **80 Beverly St** **citywinery.com/boston · $$**
This stylish wine bar features an on-site winery, a shop, and a concert space which hosts live music performances every night.

3. 1928 Beacon Hill
M3 **97 Mt Vernon St** **1928 beaconhill.com · $$**
Upscale casual dining combined with trendy cocktails attracts customers to this antiques-filled restaurant and bar. Weekend brunch is a sumptuous affair.

4. Alibi
M2 **Liberty Hotel, 215 Charles St** **alibiboston.com · $$$**
Located within the Liberty Hotel, the trendy Alibi is a good choice for cocktails. The hotel also houses Scampo, a chic restaurant with a modern Italian-accented menu.

5. The Sevens Ale House
M3 **77 Charles St**
The epitome of a local Boston bar, with dark wood, amiable patrons, a dartboard, and good pub grub.

6. Paramount
M3 **44 Charles St** **paramount boston.com · $**
Paramount is reliably good at any time of day. Breakfast is for diner-style egg classics, lunch focuses on burgers, and dinner is all about sizzling grill fare.

PRICE CATEGORIES
For a three-course meal for one with half a bottle of wine (or equivalent meal), taxes, and extra charges.

$ under $40 $$ $40–$60 $$$ over $60

---

7. Grotto
P3 **37 Bowdoin St** **L** **grotto restaurant.com · $$**
A cozy Beacon Hill fixture serving Italian-style fixed-price menus. Order a pasta dish – you won't regret it.

8. 21st Amendment
P3 **50 Bowdoin St**
This neighborhood pub near the State House is a classy spot for legislators to indulge in a tipple or two.

9. Toscano
M3 **47 Charles St** **L Mon–Fri** **toscanoboston.com · $$$**
Toscano pioneered Tuscan cooking in Beacon Hill. The restaurant's venerable kitchen works wonders with charcoal-grilled meats.

10. 75 Chestnut
M3 **75 Chestnut St** **L except Sat & Sun brunch** **75chestnut.com · $$**
Set in a converted townhouse, this restaurant serves as one of Beacon Hill's most popular hangouts for brunch and dinner. The menu offers affordable American bistro dishes.

A live performance in the concert space at City Winery

BACK BAY

The easily navigated grid of streets in Back Bay bears little resemblance to the labyrinthine lanes around Downtown and the North End. In the mid-1800s, Back Bay was filled in to accommodate Boston's mushrooming population and, by the late 1800s, the area had become a vibrant, upscale neighborhood. Home to many of Boston's wealthiest families, the area was planned along French lines, with elegant boulevards, and characterized by lavish houses, grand churches, and bustling commercial zones. Many of the original buildings stand intact, providing an exquisite 19th-century backdrop for today's pulsing nightlife, world-class shopping, and sumptuous dining. Today, Back Bay is one of Boston's most exclusive neighborhoods.

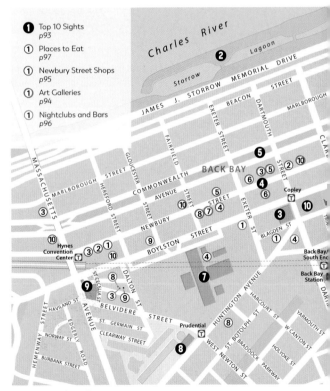

- **1** Top 10 Sights p93
- **1** Places to Eat p97
- **1** Newbury Street Shops p95
- **1** Art Galleries p94
- **1** Nightclubs and Bars p96

For places to stay in this area, see p148

1 Trinity Church

When Henry Cobb's 60-story 200 Clarendon tower was completed in 1976, Bostonians feared that Trinity Church (p40) would be overshadowed by its gleaming neighbor. Yet H. H. Richardson's masterpiece, dedicated in 1877, remains just as vital to Copley Square, and as beautiful, as it was on its opening day.

2 The Esplanade
⊡ M3

The perfect setting for a leisurely bike ride, invigorating jog, or a lazy afternoon of soaking up the sun, the Esplanade is one of the city's most

Orchestra performance at the Hatch Shell at The Esplanade

popular green spaces. It's at its busiest on the Fourth of July (p76), when the world-famous Boston Pops Orchestra plays at the Hatch Shell (p74) and thousands of revelers flock here to enjoy the incomparable mix of music, good cheer, and awe-inspiring fireworks.

3 Boston Public Library
⊡ L5 ⊡ 700 Boylston St ⊡ 9am–8pm Mon–Thu, 9am–5pm Fri & Sat, 11am–5pm Sun ⊎ bpl.org

Founded in 1848 as America's first fully public library, the Boston Public Library moved into its current location in 1895. The building, designed by McKim, Mead, & White, has lavish stone and marble interiors, gleaming oak woodwork, and murals by leading artists of the era on its walls. No wonder it's been called a "palace of the people." Take a guided tour to learn more about the building's architecture and history.

4 Newbury Street

Over the years, Back Bay's most famous street (p34) has proven to be amazingly adaptable, with fashion boutiques blending seamlessly into their mid-19th-century brownstone environs. This is the liveliest, most eclectic street in Boston: skateboarders glide alongside fashionistas, and delivery trucks and Ferraris jockey for the same parking space. Expect to hear a dozen languages on the sidewalks.

5 Commonwealth Avenue

🗺 J5–L4

With its leafy pedestrian mall and belle époque-inspired architecture, Commonwealth Avenue aptly deserves its comparison to *les rues parisiennes*. A morning jog on the mall is a popular pastime, as is the occasional picnic or afternoon stroll under the trees. Highlights include Boston's First Baptist Church (*110 Commonwealth*; open for worship) and the pedestrian mall's stately statues, including the William Lloyd Garrison bronze, sculpted by Olin Levi Warner.

6 Gibson House Museum

🗺 M4 🏠 137 Beacon St 🕐 For tours at 3pm, 4pm, & 5pm Thu; 1pm, 2pm & 3pm Fri–Sun (reserve in advance) 🌐 thegibsonhouse.org 🔗

One of the first private residences to be built in Back Bay (c. 1859), Gibson House remains beautifully intact. It has been preserved as a monument to the era, thanks largely to the efforts of its final owner, writer Charles Hammond Gibson Jr. (the grandson of the Catherine Hammond Gibson who built the house). So frozen in time does this house appear that you might feel like you're intruding on someone's inner sanctum, and an earlier age. Highlights of the tour include elegant porcelain dinnerware, 18th-century heirloom jewelry, and exquisite black walnut woodwork throughout the house. Once a month, the museum runs tours about the life of Charles Gibson.

7 Prudential Center

🗺 K6 🏠 800 Boylston St 🕐 Stores: 11am–8pm Mon–Sat, 11am–7pm Sun 🌐 prudentialcenter.com/visit

The Prudential Tower's 52 stories seem dwarfed by the huge swath of street-level shops and restaurants that constitute the Prudential Center. With its indoor shopping mall, restaurants, supermarket, cluster of residential towers, and huge convention center, the Prudential Center is like a self-contained city within a city. It is linked via a skywalk over Huntington Avenue to the Copley Place shopping and hotel complex.

8 Christian Science Plaza

🗺 K6 🏠 Corner of Huntington Ave and Massachusetts Ave 🌐 christianscience.com

At the center of this plaza is the Mother Church, a Romanesque-Byzantine basilica (open for services on Sundays). Outside, a 670-ft (204-m) reflecting pool, designed by I. M. Pei, is lined with begonias, marigolds, and columbines. The plaza is also home to the Christian Science Publishing House, which features the Mapparium™ (*p56*), a

Christian Science Plaza, with the Mother Church and reflection pool

stained-glass globe illuminated by LED lighting. The Mary Baker Eddy Library, a major scholarly resource, has a small museum dedicated to Eddy (p50) and the Christian Science religion.

9 Berklee Performance Center

J6 ⬛136 Massachusetts Ave 🌐berklee.edu/BPC

The largest independent music school in the world, Berklee was founded in 1945. The college has produced a number of world-renowned jazz, rock, and pop stars, including Quincy Jones, Melissa Etheridge, Kevin Eubanks, Jan Hammer, and Branford Marsalis. The state-of-the-art performance center hosts concerts by students, faculty, and visiting artists.

10 Copley Square

L5

Named after John Singleton Copley, the renowned 18th-century Boston painter, Copley Square is surrounded by some of the city's most striking architectural gems, notably Trinity Church and the Boston Public Library. A hub of activity, the bustling square hosts weekly farmers' markets, concerts, and folk dance shows in summer; come winter, it plays a central role in First Night (p77) activities and performances.

EXPLORING BACK BAY

Afternoon

Enjoy a *croque monsieur* or *moules frites* at the **Bistro du Midi** (272 Boylston St) while gazing out onto the **Public Garden** (p28). Stroll one block over to **Newbury Street** (p34) and take in the contemporary art galleries concentrated between Arlington and Dartmouth streets. Then cross back over to Boylston at Dartmouth and sit for a while inside **Trinity Church** (p40), where La Farge's stained-glass windows top an inexhaustible list of highlights. While you're in an aesthetics-appreciating mood, walk St. James Place to the **Fairmont Copley Plaza** hotel (138 St James Ave) and take in the ornate, Versailles-esque lobby. Next, cross Dartmouth to the **Boston Public Library** (p91) and admire John Singer Sargent's gorgeous murals.

Now it's time for a shopping spree. Turn left onto Newbury Street for Boston-only boutiques such as **Newbury Comics** (p95) and **Trident Booksellers & Café** (p95). Pause for a towering sundae at **Ben & Jerry's** (174 Newbury St). At Massachusetts Avenue, turn left, then left again onto Boylston and continue to the **Prudential Center** for name-brand shopping – you'll find Saks Fifth Avenue, Swarovski, and the like. Cap it all off with a cocktail in the elegant **City Bar** (p96) in the Lenox Hotel, an Edwardian-era survivor a block away on Exeter Street.

Art Galleries

1. Robert Klein
📍 M5 🏢 38 Newbury St 🕐 Sun & Mon
🌐 robertkleingallery.com
Everybody who's anybody in photography vies for space here. Past coups include shows by Annie Leibovitz and Herb Ritts. Open by appointment only.

2. Galerie d'Orsay
📍 M5 🏢 33 Newbury St 🌐 galerie-dorsay.com
This gallery is home to over six centuries of art, including pieces by Old Masters and Impressionists. It holds themed exhibitions, and sources new and pre-owned works by a range of artists.

3. Childs Gallery
📍 L5 🏢 168 Newbury St 🕐 Mon
🌐 childsgallery.com
The Childs Gallery was founded in 1937 and displays an eclectic range of paintings, drawings, and sculpture. Don't miss the print department in the basement.

4. Krakow Witkin Gallery
📍 M5 🏢 10 Newbury St 🕐 Sun & Mon; Aug 🌐 krakowwitkingallery.com
Since its opening in 1964, this gallery has championed contemporary artists who create conceptually driven and minimalist work.

5. DTR Modern Galleries
📍 L5 🏢 167 Newbury St 🌐 dtrmodern.com
DTR champions modern and contemporary art, ranging from Dalí to Warhol.

Sculpture outside Vose Galleries

6. Guild of Boston Artists
📍 L5 🏢 162 Newbury St 🕐 Sun & Mon
🌐 guildofbostonartists.org
The skylit gallery space houses paintings and sculptures by New England artists. More than 40 artists founded the guild in 1914.

7. Vose Galleries
📍 K5 🏢 238 Newbury St 🕐 Sun
🌐 vosegalleries.com
The oldest family-owned art gallery in the US, Vose specializes in American realist paintings and works on paper from the 18th to 20th centuries.

8. Pucker Gallery
📍 K5 🏢 240 Newbury St, 3rd floor
🌐 puckergallery.com
You never know what you might discover in this gallery. It embraces work in a variety of media created by US and international artists.

9. Gallery NAGA
📍 M5 🏢 67 Newbury St 🕐 Sun & Mon; mid-Jul–early Sep 🌐 gallerynaga.com
Representing some of New England's best-regarded artists, NAGA is possibly Newbury Street's top contemporary art gallery.

10. Arden Gallery
📍 L5 🏢 129 Newbury St 🕐 Mon
🌐 ardengallery.com
Established in 1987, this gallery focuses on original paintings and sculpture, including those cast in bronze and other metals. It also showcases up-and-coming abstract and realist artists.

The storefront of Galerie d'Orsay on Newbury Street

Newbury Street Shops

1. Johnny Cupcakes
🔁 J6 🏠 332 Newbury St

This boutique specializes in limited-edition crossbones-and-cupcake T-shirts. The cake theme continues with bakery case displays, aprons on the staff, and the smell of batter in the air.

2. Trident Booksellers & Café
🔁 J6 🏠 338 Newbury St

Trident is popular for its delicious, healthy sandwiches, strong coffee concoctions, and what is arguably the best book and magazine selection in the city.

3. Newbury Comics
🔁 J6 🏠 348 Newbury St

With a stellar selection of rare import CDs and a growing range of exclusive, rare, and vintage vinyl, this store is a must for music fans – and often good-value, too. Look out for autographed CDs and records.

4. No Rest for Bridget
🔁 K5 🏠 220 Newbury St

Youngsters flock to the Boston outpost of this Los Angeles womenswear label to pick up effortless and comfortable threads. It's a popular choice come spring break and summer vacation.

5. Hempest
🔁 K5 🏠 301 Newbury St

A true believer in the superiority of hemp as something to wear rather than inhale, Hempest showcases chic and casual styles fashioned from this environmentally friendly fiber.

6. Castanet Designer Consignment
🔁 L5 🏠 175 Newbury St

On Boston's fashion street, this shop is one of the best places to look for high-end, secondhand women's clothing.

7. Shreve, Crump, & Low
🔁 M5 🏠 39 Newbury St 🕐 Sun

First opened in 1796 near Paul Revere's silversmith shop, this fine jeweler is a Boston institution, renowned for its engagement rings. The so-called "gurgling cod" jugs make a whimsical and less pricey gift.

8. Concepts
🔁 J6 🏠 18 Newbury St

An impressive collection of sneakers, street wear, and designer clothing, ranging from Adidas to Jimmy Choo, is stocked here.

9. Simon Pearce
🔁 L5 🏠 103 Newbury St

Here, the eponymous Irish designer and artist creates tableware with an upscale touch: fine blown glass, handmade pottery, and the like. Pearce's signatures include classic goblets and other stemware.

10. Deluca's Back Bay Market
🔁 K5 🏠 239 Newbury St

This grocer-meets-corner market stocks tasty produce, chilled beer, ready-made sandwiches, and imported delights of all kinds. It's a great option for picking up a few picnic supplies.

Colorful stalls of produce for sale at Deluca's Back Bay Market

Nightclubs and Bars

Enjoying a game of ten-pin bowling at Kings

1. City Bar
⊡ L5 ⬚ 65 Exeter St ⬚ To 2am daily
A world away from the hubbub of Back Bay, City Bar, housed in the Lenox Hotel, is a sophisticated choice. The interior is all dark wood and leather seating, creating a glamorous vibe.

2. OAK Long Bar + Kitchen
⊡ M5 ⬚ 138 St James Ave
This award-winning bar in the historic Copley Plaza exudes old-school class and charm.

3. Kings
⊡ K6 ⬚ 50 Dalton St
The 1950s were never as cool as they seem at this retro-style lounge, pool hall, and bowling alley buried downstairs next to the Hynes Convention Center.

4. Bar 10
⊡ L5 ⬚ 10 Huntington Ave
The Westin Copley Place's lobby bar has cozy booths, perfect for a leisurely drink, while the high top tables are a great choice for quick sips and rendezvous.

5. M.J. O'Connor's
⊡ N5 ⬚ 27 Columbus Ave
Located in the Park Plaza Hotel, this expansive Irish-style pub features a full bar, complete with the ubiquitous Guinness plus several local brews. It serves comfort food, too.

6. The Street Bar
⊡ M4 ⬚ The Newbury, 1 Newbury St ⬚ 11:30pm or 12:30am Fri & Sat
Boston's elite have been socializing at this hideaway facing the Public Garden since the Prohibition ended.

7. Bijou Nightclub
⊡ N5 ⬚ 51 Stuart St
High rollers reserve a table at Bijou to enjoy a glass of champagne, but most of the crowd come to dance to the Latin and House beats.

8. Bukowski Tavern
⊡ K6 ⬚ 50 Dalton St
A beer drinker's paradise, Bukowski counts 100 varieties of the beverage. Its primary patrons are a professional crowd during the day and young hipsters at night.

9. Hecate
⊡ K5 ⬚ 48 Gloucester St
Named after the goddess of magic and spells, this underground bar is known for its stunning cocktails. Try the Undertow, which includes Hawaiian agricole rum mingled with black kumquat and spirulina.

10. Dillon's
⊡ K5 ⬚ 955 Boylston St
Set in a former police station, Dillon's serves an all-American menu and drinks. The interior of this bi-level bar is impressive, but the outdoor patio is hard to beat in good weather.

Places to Eat

1. Sorellina

L5 **1 Huntington Ave** **sorellina boston.com** · **$$$**

Regional Italian food with a contemporary spin is accompanied by a range of great wines in this chic dining room.

2. Saltie Girl

L5 **279 Dartmouth St** **saltiegirl. com** · **$$$**

Inspired by Barcelona's seafood bars, Saltie Girl offers delicious dishes made with local fish. The restaurant serves a variety of excellent cocktails.

3. Deuxave

J5 **371 Commonwealth Ave** **L** **deuxave.com** · **$$$**

Elegant contemporary dining with dishes ranging from local lobster to caramelized onion ravioli.

4. Eataly

K6 **800 Boylston St** **eataly.com** · **$–$$$**

This vast emporium of all things Italian includes more than a dozen dining venues and shelves stocked with groceries and kitchen gadgets.

5. The Banks Fish House

M5 **406 Stuart St** **L Sat & Sun** **thebanksboston.com** · **$$$**

Popular fish house that stays true to Boston's maritime heritage. Everything is delicious, from the broiled lobster to the herb-crusted halibut.

6. Mistral

M6 **223 Columbus Ave** **mistral bistro.com** · **$$$**

Delectable French-Mediterranean dishes and an excellent wine list make Mistral an ideal dining venue.

7. Grill 23 & Bar

M5 **161 Berkeley St** **L** **grill23. com** · **$$$**

Grill 23 harkens back to the days of exclusive, Prohibition-era supper clubs. Prime aged beef with an inventive spin is served in a sumptuously classic interior.

PRICE CATEGORIES

For a three-course meal for one with half a bottle of wine (or equivalent meal), taxes, and extra charges.

$ under $40 $$ $40–$60 $$$ over $60

8. Lucie Drink + Dine

K6 **120 Huntington Ave** **luciebackbay.com** · **$$**

Serving everything from steak and fries to rice bowls, the Colonnade Hotel's stylish restaurant specializes in comfort food from all around the globe.

9. Summer Shack

K6 **50 Dalton St** **summershack restaurant.com** · **$$**

Boston celebrity chef Jasper White serves excellent dishes at the Summer Shack. Make sure to try the buttered lobster and corn.

10. Uni

J5 **370A Commonwealth Ave** **L & Mon** **uni-boston.com** · **$$$**

Contemporary Japanese cuisine rules at this lively, fine-dining *izakaya* restaurant. Late-night weekend ramen draws a crowd.

The lower level at the Banks Fish House in Back Bay

NORTH END AND THE WATERFRONT

One of Boston's oldest neighborhoods, the North End wears its history with pride. The steeple of Old North Church literally lit the way for the American Revolution. A century later, the language echoing through the area's narrow streets was Italian. The North End retains its Italian identity, although most immigrants have since moved on. The area along the waterfront, meanwhile, has seen much development, with condo developments and the city's aquarium springing up on former shipping piers.

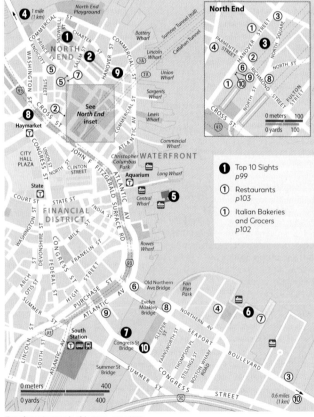

Top 10 Sights
p99

Restaurants
p103

Italian Bakeries and Grocers
p102

For places to stay in this area, see p149

1 Copp's Hill Burying Ground

Q1 ❚ Hull St ☎ (617) 635-7361
🕓 9am–4pm daily

Trace the history of Boston on the thousands of tombstones found here, from the mean-spirited Mather family, who were theocrats who ruled the early city of the late 17th and 18th centuries, to the valiant patriots slain in the fight for freedom during the American Revolution. In the Battle of Bunker Hill (p24), the British, who occupied the city in 1775, manned a battery from this site and fired on neighboring Charlestown. There are sweeping views of the harbor.

2 Old North Church

Q1 ❚ 193 Salem St 🕓 11am–5pm Tue–Sat, 12:30pm–5pm Sun
🌐 oldnorth.com

An active Episcopal congregation still worships at Boston's oldest church, officially known as Christ Church (1723). It was here, in 1775, that sexton Robert Newman hung two lanterns in the belfry to warn horseback messenger Paul Revere

The clapboard exterior of the Paul Revere House

of British troop movements, an event commemorated by a bronze plaque in the street outside.

3 Paul Revere House

Q1 ❚ 19 North Sq 🕓 Mid-Apr–Oct: 10am–5:15pm daily; Nov–mid-Apr: 10am–4:15pm daily 🕓 Jan–Mar: Mon 🌐 paul reverehouse.org

Home to Paul Revere for 30 years, this 17th-century clapboard house is the only surviving home of one of Boston's key revolutionary figures. It provides an intriguing glimpse into the domestic life of Revere's family with displays of their furniture and possessions, including silverwork made by Revere, who was highly regarded as a metalsmith. Well-informed staff tell the tale of Revere's legendary midnight ride (p24).

4 Charlestown Navy Yard

One of the original six naval yards created to support the fledgling US Navy, the Charlestown Navy Yard (p44) was established in 1800 as a center of technical innovation until its decommissioning in 1974. The facility was transferred to the National Park Service to interpret the art and history of naval shipbuilding. Today, the two most popular exhibits here are the famous USS *Constitution* frigate, which was christened in 1797, and the World War II–era steel destroyer USS *Cassin Young*.

The interior of Old North Church on Salem Street

The harborside setting of the Boston Tea Party Ships and Museum

5 New England Aquarium

Now the centerpiece of the downtown waterfront development, the aquarium (p46) was constructed in the 1960s and paved the way for the revitalization of Boston Harbor. Harbor seals cavort in a tank in front of the sleek structure.

6 Institute of Contemporary Art

🅰 25 Harbor Shore Dr 🕙 10am–5pm Tue, Wed, Sat, & Sun, 10am–9pm Thu & Fri 🌐 icaboston.org 🔗

The ICA was founded in 1936 and reopened in its modern landmark structure on Fan Pier in 2006. The striking glass, wood, and steel building, designed by Diller Scofidio + Renfro, is cantilevered over the Harborwalk and provides dramatic views. The ICA promotes cutting-edge art and focuses on 21st-century work. There is also a good program of performing arts and other events, with waterfront concerts in summer.

7 Boston Tea Party Ships and Museum

🚇 R5 🅰 Congress St Bridge 🕙 10am–4pm daily 🌐 bostonteapartyship.com 🔗

On the historic occasion of the Boston Tea Party, patriots dressed as Indigenous people and threw a consignment of English tea overboard to protest against the Stamp Tax of 1773 – this became a catalyst of the American Revolution (p9). The Boston Tea Party ships are replicas of the vessels that were relieved of their cargo that fateful December night, including two British East India Company ships anchored on the Fort Point Channel, a short distance south of the original wharf site. Costumed storytellers recount events in rousing detail, and visitors can board one of the vessels and even participate in a reenactment of the destruction. In the museum is one of two tea crates known to have survived from the incident. Abigail's Tea Room serves up a nice "cuppa."

8 Rose Kennedy Greenway

🚇 Q2 🌐 rosekennedygreenway.org

The Greenway is a ribbon of parkland that runs through the heart of Boston. Here visitors and locals laze on the lawns, cool off in the fountains, buy lunch at one of the food trucks, and enjoy seasonal beer and wine gardens. There's a charming carousel featuring local hand-carved wildlife, too. Artworks include the Harbor Fog water sculpture, near Rowes Wharf, which evokes the sea with fog, light, and sound, and installations that change every year. Colorful garden plants punctuate the park's meandering walkways.

9 St. Stephen's Church

R1 **401 Hanover St** **(617) 523-1230** **For services 7:30am Thu–Fri, 4pm Sat, 11am Sun**

Renowned architect Charles Bulfinch completely redesigned St. Stephen's original 1714 structure in 1802–4, and the church is the only surviving example of his religious architecture. The Neo-Classical exterior contrasts with the relatively unadorned interior. In 1862, the Roman Catholic archdiocese took over the church to accommodate the growing number of Irish immigrants. Rose Fitzgerald, daughter of Boston mayor and St. Stephen's parishioner John "Honey Fitz" Fitzgerald, and mother of President John F. Kennedy (p51), is linked to the church. It was here that she was baptized in 1890 and remembered at her funeral in 1995.

10 Children's Museum

R5 **308 Congress St** bostonchildrensmuseum.org

This huge interactive museum is the perfect place to take the family for hands-on fun.

Kids climbing the labyrinth at the Children's Museum

FROM NARROW BYWAYS TO THE SEA

Trade
525 yards (480 meters)

Morning

From the Haymarket "T", follow Hanover Street to Richmond Street and continue to North Square. Stop at **Paul Revere House** (p99) for a glimpse into the life of a key revolutionary figure. Return to Hanover for an espresso at **Caffè Vittoria** (p70). Continue up Hanover and turn left through Paul Revere Mall to **Old North Church** (p99). Inside, the bust of George Washington is reputedly the world's most accurate rendering of his face. Stroll up Hull Street past **Copp's Hill Burying Ground** (p99) for a great view of USS *Constitution* (p44) and continue to the waterfront. Grab a bench in **Langone Park** (p53) to watch a match of bocce. Walk south along Commercial Street and stop for lunch at **Joe's Waterfront** (100 Atlantic Ave).

Afternoon

Resume your waterfront stroll, admiring the views of the harbor as you walk. Then stop off to enjoy the roses in the **Rose Kennedy Greenway**, before whiling away an hour in the **New England Aquarium** (p46) where highlights include the swirling Giant Ocean Tank. Relax with a sundowner on the patio of the **Boston Harbor Hotel** (p149) before you head to **Trade** (p103) for dinner.

Italian Bakeries and Grocers

1. Mike's Pastry
🅰 Q1 📍 300 Hanover St

Large glass cases display a huge selection of cookies and cannoli (crunchy pastry filled with a sweet ricotta cream). Purchase a box to go, or grab a table and enjoy your pastry with a cup of coffee.

2. Salumeria Italiana
🅰 Q2 📍 151 Richmond St

This neighborhood fixture is a great source of esoteric Italian canned goods and rich olive oils, as well as spicy sausages and cheeses from many Italian regions.

3. The Wine Bottega
🅰 Q2 📍 341 Hanover St

Run by wine connoisseurs, The Wine Bottega only stocks natural wines, which are made with no chemical input in the vineyard or the winery. Prices run the gamut, from the wallet-friendly to investment pieces that might one day be opened at a special occasion.

4. Polcari's Coffee Co.
🅰 Q1 📍 105 Salem St 🕐 Sun

The premier bulk grocer in the North End, this charming store has sold fine Italian roasted coffee since 1932. It's still the best place to find spices, flours, grains, and legumes.

5. Bova's Bakery
🅰 Q1 📍 134 Salem St

Head here for hot sandwiches, cookies, and bread, which is fresh and baked at all hours of the day.

6. Modern Pastry
🅰 Q2 📍 257 Hanover St

The house specialties here include a rich ricotta pie and delicious florentines, which are made on the premises, as well as chocolate truffles from Italy. Some cannoli fans swear by Modern's delicate shells.

A wide selection of coffee beans at Polcari's Coffee Co.

7. Monica's Mercato
🅰 Q1 📍 130 Salem St

Linked to a nearby restaurant, this *salumeria* has all the usual cheeses and sausages, but its specialties are prepared foods such as cold salads and pasta dishes.

8. V. Cirace Wine & Spirits
🅰 Q2 📍 173 North St 🕐 Sun

The North End's most upscale seller of Italian wines and liqueurs was established in 1906 and continues to be run by the same family. It stocks both fine wines to lay down and cheerfully youthful ones to enjoy right away.

9. Bricco Panetteria
🅰 Q2 📍 241 Hanover St

This subterranean bakery turns out amazing Italian and French breads day and night. Follow the delicious smells to find it tucked down an alley, behind Bricco Ristorante.

10. Bricco Salumeria & Pasta Shop
🅰 Q2 📍 11 Board Alley

With many varieties of fresh pasta made daily, plus sauces, pesto, grating cheeses, and a handful of hard-to-find Italian groceries, this North End takeout is ideal for stocking up a picnic basket – Rose Kennedy Greenway is nearby.

Restaurants

1. Mare Oyster Bar
Q2 223 Hanover St mareoysterbar.com · $$$

Savor Italian coastal cuisine at this sleek contemporary spot, which offers a variety of crudos, a never-ending supply of oysters, and shellfish, as well as some of the best organic white wines.

2. Neptune Oyster
Q1 63 Salem St neptuneoyster.com · $$$

The delicate raw bar oysters are almost upstaged by large and bold roasted fish and rice dishes in this tiny, stylish spot. Tables turn quickly.

3. Legal Harborside
Liberty Wharf and other locations legalseafoods.com · $$$

The flagship of the Legal Sea Foods chain, Legal Harborside offers three floors of seafood heaven.

4. Strega Italiano Seaport
H4 1 Marina Park Dr stregaitaliano.com · $$$

Italian by way of the Jersey Shore, this Tuscan steakhouse celebrates bold flavors and tannic red wines.

5. Regina Pizzeria
Q1 11½ Thatcher St regina-pizza.co.uk · $

This original, family-run branch bakes thin-crust, old-fashioned, Neapolitan-style pizzas in its brick oven.

6. James Hook & Co.
R4 440 Atlantic Avenue D jameshooklobster.com · $$

This place has earned widespread acclaim for its flavorful lobster rolls, clam chowder, and stuffed clams.

7. Woods Hill Pier 4
300 Pier 4 Blvd woodshillpier4.com · $$$

Lending a creative twist to classic New England cuisine, this American

chophouse uses ingredients fresh from its organic farm. It also offers unparalleled waterfront views.

8. Barking Crab
H4 88 Sleeper St barkingcrab.com · $$

Located next to the Children's Museum, this casual waterfront restaurant is one of the city's favorite spots for seafood and drinks.

9. Trade
Q4 540 Atlantic Ave trade-boston.com · $$$

This airy upscale restaurant evokes Boston's global shipping days with its superb, eclectic Mediterranean cuisine. There's also a great selection of creative cocktails.

10. Chickadee
21 Dry Doch Ave L chickadeerestaurant.com · $$

A cheerful restaurant sporting a sleek and modern vibe. The menu abounds with light Mediterranean fare, such as octopus *escabeche* and slow-roasted *porchetta*.

Diners enjoying a night out at the Barking Crab

DOWNTOWN AND THE FINANCIAL DISTRICT

The heart of Boston lies between Boston Common and the harbor. There are reminders of history embedded in the center of this metropolis. The 18th-century Old State House still shines within a canyon of skyscrapers and the major figures of Boston's early years – John Winthrop, Paul Revere, and Samuel Adams – are buried just steps from sidewalks abuzz with shoppers. Rolled in to this area is the Financial District and Boston's oldest commercial district, Faneuil Hall Marketplace.

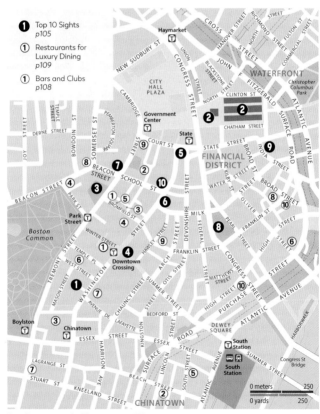

- **1** Top 10 Sights
  p105
- **1** Restaurants for Luxury Dining
  p109
- **1** Bars and Clubs
  p108

For places to stay in this area, see p149

Brattle Book Shop, Ladder District

1 Ladder District

◘ P4

The network of short streets linking Washington and Tremont streets is today known as the Ladder District. Once derelict, the area is now filled with bars and restaurants. Anchoring the district are the Millennium Tower, which overlooks Boston Common (p28), the Ritz-Carlton, and the top-of-the-line AMC Boston Common cineplex (175 Tremont St). A few stalwarts, such as landmark bookseller Brattle Book Shop, hold out against the large nationwide chains.

2 Faneuil Hall Marketplace

◘ Q2 ◘ 1 Faneuil Hall Sq ◘ Faneuil Hall: 10am–9pm Mon–Sat, 11am–7pm Sun; Quincy Market: hours vary, chech website **ⓦ** faneuilhall marketplace.com

Faneuil Hall is a historic Boston landmark where, in the early to mid-18th century, enslaved people were auctioned. During the second half of the 18th century, this hall echoed with cries of revolution. The adjacent Quincy Market revolutionized Boston's food distribution in the 1820s. Today, the buildings and surrounding plazas form a shopping and dining hub called the Faneuil Hall Marketplace, attracting nearly 18 million people every year.

3 Old Granary Burying Ground

◘ P3 ◘ Tremont St at Park St **◖** (617) 635-4505 **◘** 9am–4pm daily

Dating from 1660, the Granary has the graves of many illustrious figures, including John Hancock, Samuel Adams, and Paul Revere (p50). There are other notable people such as the parents of Benjamin Franklin, and Crispus Attucks, a freedom seeker who was the first casualty of the Boston Massacre (p24).

4 Downtown Crossing

◘ P4 ◘ Junction of Summer, Winter, & Washington sts

This pedestrian-friendly shopping area is dominated by Macy's department store. Pushcart vendors offer more quirky goods, and food carts provide quick lunches for Downtown office workers.

5 Old State House

◘ Q3 ◘ Washington & State sts **◘** 10am–5pm daily **ⓦ** revolutionary spaces.org **◘**

Built in 1713 as the seat of colonial government, the Old State House saw the Boston Massacre (p24) occurr outside its doors in 1770. In July 1776, the Declaration of Independence was first read from its balcony. Today, it's home to a museum dedicated to Boston's Revolutionary era.

The airy interior of King's Chapel on Tremont Street

6 Old South Meeting House

🔲 Q3 🏠 310 Washington St
🕙 10am–5pm daily 🌐 revolutionary
spaces.org 🔲

Old South's rafters have rung with many impassioned speeches exhorting the overthrow of the king, the abolition of slavery, women's right to vote, an end to apartheid, and many other causes. Nearly abandoned when its congregation moved to Back Bay in 1876, it was saved in one of Boston's first acts of preservation.

7 King's Chapel

🔲 P3 🏠 58 Tremont St 🕙 10am–5pm Mon–Sat; check website for winter hours; recitals: 12:15pm Tue 🌐 kings-chapel.org 🔲

The first Anglican Church in Puritan Boston was established in 1686 to serve British Army officers. When Anglicans fled Boston along with British forces in 1776, the chapel became the first Unitarian Church in the Americas. The church is known for its program of classical concerts.

8 Post Office Square

🔲 Q3

On a sunny day this green oasis in the heart of the Financial District is filled with office workers who claim a bench or a spot of grass for a picnic. Surrounding the park are some of the area's most architecturally distinctive buildings, including the Art Deco post office *(Congress St)*, the Renaissance Revival former Federal Reserve building (now the Langham, Boston hotel, *p149*), and the Art Moderne New England Telephone Building *(185 Franklin St)*.

9 Custom House

🔲 Q3 🏠 3 McKinley Sq 📞 (617) 310-6300 🕙 Tower: 2pm Sat–Thu by reservation 🔲

When the Custom House was built in 1840, Boston was one of America's largest overseas shipping ports, and customs fees were the mainstay of the Federal budget. Before landfill altered the downtown topography, the Neo-Classical structure once sat on the waterfront, but now stands two

blocks inland. The 16-story Custom House tower, added in 1913, was Boston's first skyscraper. Since the 1990s, peregrine falcons have nested in the clock tower under the watchful eyes of wildlife biologists. Tours of the tower give views of the harbor. A bar service is available on evening tours.

10 Old Corner Bookstore
 P3 1 School St

Built in 1729, this enduring spot on the Freedom Trail remains one of the most tangible sites associated with the writers of the New England Renaissance of the last half of the 19th century. Both the *Atlantic Monthly* magazine and Ticknor & Fields (publishers of Ralph Waldo Emerson and Henry David Thoreau) made this modest structure their headquarters during the mid- and late 19th century, when Boston was the literary, intellectual, and publishing center of the country. The latter is often credited with carving out the first distinctively American literature. Saving the site from demolition in 1960 led to the formation of Historic Boston Incorporated. The building, however, is no longer connected to publishing, but is instead used for retail space and commercial businesses.

The historic buildings and skyscrapers of downtown Boston

A SHOPPING SPREE

Morning
The "T" will deposit you at Downtown Crossing, where you can shop the fashions and accessories of **Macy's** (*450 Washington St*) at leisure. Then proceed over to **DSW Shoe Warehouse** (*385 Washington St*) for a great selection of shoes at discount prices. Make a left up Bromfield Street to peruse the fine writing implements and elegant stationery at **Bromfield Pen Shop** (*49 Bromfield St*). The walk to Quincy Market down Franklin Street will take you past the Financial District with its tall and imposing skyscrapers. Turn left at **Post Office Square** for lunch at **Sip Café** (*Post Office Square Park*).

Afternoon
Stop to enjoy a short rest outside **Faneuil Hall Marketplace** (*p105*) before you begin your spree in earnest. Numerous name-brand shops await and if you want to bag a souvenir, or a New England sweatshirt, head to the Black Dog. Then pay a visit to **Irish Eyes** (*1 S Market St*) for Emerald Isle-inspired souvenirs. Have an early dinner and take in the scene at an outdoor table at **Salty Dog Seafood Grille & Bar** (*Quincy Market*). Order fried seafood, Maine lobster, or a complete shore meal. After dinner, savor a pint while enjoying live music at **The Black Rose** (*160 State St*).

Beantown Pub on Tremont Street

Bars and Clubs

1. Beantown Pub
P3 **100 Tremont St**
This no-frills tourist hangout is filled with numerous pool tables and even more TVs, all of which are tuned to big sports games and events.

2. Corner Pub
P5 **162 Lincoln St**
Located in the Leather District, this friendly bar and grill serves excellent cocktails and a wide selection of draft beers to go with good burgers.

3. Haley.Henry Wine Bar
P3 **45 Province St**
This nautical-themed wine bar, housed in a chic condo building, specializes in natural wines and tinned fish from Spain and Portugal. The menu also features cheese and small plates of ceviche and charcuterie.

4. Side Bar
P3 **14 Bromfield St**
Probably the least expensive spot to be found near Downtown Crossing, Side Bar has giant TV screens airing sports constantly, an arcade, and a snazzy jukebox.

5. Silvertone Bar & Grill
P3 **69 Bromfield St**
A surprisingly unpretentious, contemporary beer bar and casual restaurant, Silvertone is a great place for good,
reasonably priced comfort food and drinks. The creamy mac and cheese is excellent.

6. JM Curley
P4 **21 Temple Pl**
Named for Boston's old-time felonious mayor, this bar has good pub food (served until late) and an exhaustive list of craft and mass-market beers.

7. The Tam
P3 **222 Tremont St**
A local favorite, this cozy, brightly lit dive bar (cash only) serves cheap beer and generous pours of liquor.

8. Carrie Nation Cocktail Club
P3 **11 Beacon St** **Mon**
This sleek, 1920s-inspired speakeasy slings up complex cocktails from Tuesday to Saturday, while Sunday is reserved for a raucous drag brunch.

9. The Merchant
P4 **60 Franklin St**
A spacious American brasserie, The Merchant is a popular choice for its huge beer list, creative cocktails, and menu of savory bar bites.

10. Broadside Tavern
Q3 **99 Broad St**
This pub is the ultimate spot for people to chat, watch sports together, and discuss current news.

Restaurants for Luxury Dining

1. Yvonne's
P4 **2 Winter Pl** **L** **yvonnes boston.com · $$$**
A modern twist to the concept of a supper club, Yvonne's dishes up contemporary American fare and a well-chosen collection of wines and cocktails.

2. Ruth's Chris Steak House
P3 **45 School St** **L Sat–Thu** **ruthschris.com/boston · $$$**
Classy steak emporium located in the historic Old City Hall building. Fine service and a top-notch wine list.

3. blu
P4 **4 Avery St** **Sun** **blu restaurant.com · $$$**
Light, fresh, and artistically presented international cuisine is complemented by the restaurant's soaring Post-Modern architecture.

4. No. 9 Park
P3 **9 Park St** **Mon & Tue** **no9 parh.com · $$$**
Hobnob with Beacon Hill highflyers in this bold bistro overlooking Boston Common, where Mediterranean flavors meet an imaginative wine list.

5. O Ya
Q5 **9 East St** **Sun & Mon** **o-ya.restaurant · $$$**
One of the city's priciest and fanciest restaurants, serving modern Japanese creations. Close to South Station.

6. The Palm
R4 **1 International Pl** **thepalm. com · $$$**
The glamorous club-like setting here matches prime beef and top-quality seafood with a broad wine list.

7. Legal Crossing
P3 **558 Washington St** **legal seafoods.com · $$$**
Yet another popular offshoot of the iconic local Legal Sea Foods empire

(p103), serving exceptionally fresh seafood, as always, along with cool, Downtown-influenced cocktails.

8. Fin Point Oyster Bar and Grill
Q3 **89 Broad St** **finpoint restaurant.com · $$$**
With its luxurious leather upholstery, glittering mirrors, and wall-height windows, this spot near the Financial District is great for a Boston seafood dinner.

9. The Oceanaire Seafood Room
Q3 **40 Court St** **theoceanaire. com · $$$**
This former bank retains its marble glamour in its current role as an outstanding seafood restaurant, with a superb raw bar and regional, seasonal dishes on the menu.

10. Society on High
Q4 **99 High St** **Sat & Sun** **societyboston.com · $$**
Smart and contemporary, this bistro offers New England specialties, alongside good tapas and cocktails. The lobster poached in butter is heavenly.

The dining room at Legal Crossing on Washington Street

CHINATOWN, THE THEATER DISTRICT, AND SOUTH END

Boston's compact Chinatown is one of the oldest and most significant in the US, concentrating a wealth of Asian experience in a small patch of real estate. It's also the third-largest Chinatown in the nation (after San Francisco and New York). Theatergoers find the proximity of Chinatown to the Theater District a boon for pre- and post-show dining. The Theater District itself is among the liveliest in the US, and its architecturally distinctive playhouses are nearly always active, often with local productions.

Adjoining the Theater District to the south is South End, once an immigrant tenement area and now Boston's most diverse neighborhood, with strong LGBTQ+ and Latin American communities. It is also the country's largest historical district of Victorian townhouses. Following decades of gentrification and inflation of real estate prices, South End is now home to a burgeoning, energetic club, café, and restaurant scene.

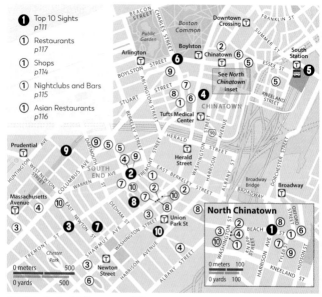

1	Top 10 Sights	p111
1	Restaurants	p117
1	Shops	p114
1	Nightclubs and Bars	p115
1	Asian Restaurants	p116

For places to stay in this area, see p150

The three-story gateway standing at the entrance to Chinatown

1 Beach Street and Chinatown

🗺 P5

As the periphery of Chinatown becomes increasingly homogenized, Beach Street remains the purely Chinese heart of the neighborhood. An ornate Dragon Gate at the base of the street creates a ceremonial entrance to Chinatown. Residents gather to socialize and play cards at the tables located in the small park adjacent to the gate.

2 Boston Center for the Arts

🗺 F5 🏛 539 Tremont St 🌐 boston arts.org

The massive Cyclorama building is the centerpiece of the Boston Center for the Arts (BCA), a performing and visual arts complex dedicated to nurturing new talent. The center provides studio space to about 40 artists, and its Mills Gallery mounts rotating visual arts exhibitions. The BCA's four theaters host avant-garde productions of dance, theater, and performance art.

3 Tremont Street

🗺 N5–M6

The part of Tremont Street between East Berkeley and Massachusetts Avenue is the social and commercial heart of the South End. Many of the handsome brick and brownstone townhouses have been restored to perfection, some with a boutique or café added at street level. The liveliest corner of the South End is the intersection of Tremont with Clarendon and Union Park streets, where the Boston Center for the Arts and a plethora of restaurants and cafés create a compact entertainment and dining district.

4 Boch Center – Wang Theatre

🗺 N5 🏛 270 Tremont St 🌐 boch center.org

With a theater modeled on the Paris Opera House and a foyer inspired by the Palace of Versailles, the opulent Wang Theatre, opened in 1925, is a grand venue for touring musicals, blockbuster concerts, and local productions.

The soaring exterior of the Boch Center – Wang Theatre

South Station's imposing Neo-Classical facade

5 South Station
Q5

A temple to mass transportation, the Neo-Classical Revival South Station was erected in 1898 at the height of rail travel in the US, and was once the country's busiest train station. Following restoration in 1989, it now serves as an Amtrak terminal for trains from the south and west of the city, as well as a "T" stop. It is also a social and commercial center with a food court and occasional free lunchtime concerts.

6 Piano Row
N4

During the late 19th century, the headquarters of leading piano makers Steinert; Vose; Starck; Mason & Hamlin; and Wurlitzer were all located on the section of Boylston Street facing Boston Common, giving the block (now a historic district) its nickname Piano Row. Over a century later, those Beaux Arts buildings still echo with music. The ornate Emerson Colonial Theatre opened in December 1900 and is the city's oldest theater in continuous operation. It is owned and managed by Emerson College and it mainly hosts touring shows. Another attraction on Piano Row is Boylston Place, a small-scale club and nightlife center.

7 Villa Victoria
F6 Area bounded by Shawmut Ave, Tremont St, W Newton St, & W Broohline St ibaboston.org

Villa Victoria is a virtually self-contained, primarily Hispanic neighborhood that grew out of a unique collaboration among Puerto Rican community activists, flexible city planners, and visionary architects. With its low-rise buildings, narrow streets, and mom-and-pop stores, Villa Victoria replicates the feel of Puerto Rican community life. It sponsors music, dance, and visual arts programs, and in mid-July, puts on the Latin American arts and cultural celebration Festival Betances.

8 Union Park
F6

Constructed between 1857 and 1859, this small park surrounded by English-style brick row townhouses was built to contrast with the French-inspired grid layout of nearby Back Bay. Graced with lovely trees and fountains and verdant with a thick mat of grass, Union Square was one of the first areas in the South End to be gentrified. Today, it's hailed as the best-preserved residential square in the area.

9 Southwest Corridor Park

E5

The first section of the 5-mile (8-km) Southwest Corridor Park divides South End and Back Bay along the "T" orange line corridor. In the residential South End portion, a path strings together numerous small parks. Between Massachusetts Avenue and West Roxbury, the park broadens to include amenities such as tennis and basketball courts.

10 Holy Cross Cathedral

F6 **1400 Washington St** **9am–6pm daily** **boston cathedral.com**

Holy Cross, the largest Roman Catholic church in Massachusetts, acts as the seat of the archbishop of Boston. The cathedral was constructed between 1866 and 1875 (on the site of the municipal gallows) to serve the largely Irish American workers who lived in the adjoining shantytown. Today the congregation is principally of Hispanic origin. Once you step inside, of note are the magnificent stained-glass windows, which include rare colored glass imported from Munich in the 19th century, and the powerful Hook & Hastings organ which, when played with the stops out, seems to make every piece of Roxbury puddingstone in the building reverberate.

Interior of the Holy Cross Cathedral on Washington Street

EXPLORING CHINATOWN AND SOUTH END

Morning

Begin on Washington Street and peruse Chinese specialty foods at **Jia Ho** (p114). Continue down Essex Street, ducking into **Oxford Place** to see the mural, *Travelers in an Autumn Landscape*, based on the scroll painting of the same name at the Museum of Fine Arts. Close by on Oxford Street is the *Where We Belong* mural by local artist Ponnapa Prakkamakul, while at the corner of Edinboro and Beach streets stands the **Dragon Gate** to **Chinatown**. Continue to the corner of Essex and Chauncy where **Essex Corner** (p114) offers a wide range of goods. Stop for lunch at **Shabu-Zen** (p116).

Afternoon

Walk down **Tremont Street** (p111) to the South End, or hop on the "T" two stops to Back Bay Station. Head west on Columbus Avenue to see the bronze sculptures that tell the story of freedom seeker Harriet Tubman, who led many enslaved people to freedom on the Underground Railroad. Back at Tremont Street, visit the **Boston Center for the Arts** (p111) to get a snapshot of local contemporary art. Stroll around the charming **Union Park** before returning to the arts center for dinner and live jazz music at **The Beehive** (p115).

Shops

Bamboo plants for sale at Essex Corner in Chinatown

1. Jia Ho Supermarket
P5 ⌂ 692 Washington St
This compact market offers a wide variety of vegetables, tropical fruits, and packaged foods – all the essentials for creating equally diverse Asian dishes.

2. Flock
N6 ⌂ 274 Shawmut Ave
Flock sells stylish and easy-to-wear women's clothing and accessories with a modern boho flair, plus an eclectic range of gifts and affordable home decor items.

3. Hudson
F6 ⌂ 12 Union Park St ◌ Sun & Mon
This home decor boutique offers home furnishings and a delightfully eclectic mix of decorative accent pieces that includes traditional, country, vintage, and modern items.

4. Lekker Home
G6 ⌂ 38 Wareham St ◌ Sun
Contemporary Italian, Scandinavian, and German home design items are the highlights of this emporium showroom, which offers the latest trends in homeware. The smaller items, such as vases and throw pillows, are perfect for adding a splash of color and style to your home.

5. Tadpole
M6 ⌂ 58 Clarendon St ◌ Mon & Sun
Tadpole's cheery selection of clothing, toys, and accessories for children are a favorite among the locals. Limited edition strollers are very popular.

6. Essex Corner
P5 ⌂ 50 Essex St
If you're looking for the perfect souvenier, Essex Corner is a great place to start. This large shop gathers all the Asian merchandise found in Chinatown into one easy-to-peruse location.

7. Michele Mercaldo Jewelry
F6 ⌂ 276 Shawmut Ave ◌ Sun & Mon
Jewelry by contemporary designer Michele Mercaldo and her colleagues is displayed in creative and unusual ways at this South End store.

8. Boston Fiber Company
G6 ⌂ 61 Thayer St ◌ Mon & Tue
A must-visit for ardent knitters, this cozy shop works with independent dyers to source all sorts of colorful yarn for your next project.

9. Urban Grape
M6 ⌂ 303 Columbus Ave
This stylish award-winning liquor store uses "progressive shelving," a unique system of organizing wines by their body instead of region or variety to make it easy for customers to select wines.

10. Formaggio Kitchen- South End
G5 ⌂ 268 Shawmut Ave
A jewel box of a gourmet shop, Formaggio Kitchen specializes in sourcing and aging small-production cheeses. This unique shop also sells charcuterie, fresh breads from local bakeries, hard-to-get spices, beer, and wine. Check out its coffee bar for a fresh cup of the good stuff, too.

Nightclubs and Bars

1. Candibar Boston

G5 ⬛ 275 Tremont St ⬛ Mon–Wed
⬛ candibarboston.com ⬛

The neon lights, creative cocktails, and glam, futuristic decor, Candibar attracts a diverse crowd.

2. Sip Wine Bar and Kitchen

P5 ⬛ 581 Washington St ⬛ Mon

This wine bar serves small plates accompanied by an excellent variety of wines, offered by the bottle or glass.

3. Wally's Café

E6 ⬛ 427 Massachusetts Ave

Exhale before you squeeze in the door at Wally's. This thin, chock-full sliver of a room is one of the best jazz bars in Boston, and has been since 1944.

4. Five Horses Tavern

F6 ⬛ 535 Columbus Ave ⬛ fivehorses tavern.com

This atmospheric, brick-walled tavern has an impressive collection of craft beers from around the world. It also serves fine whiskeys and American comfort food.

5. Delux Café

M6 ⬛ 100 Chandler St ⬛ Mon

Cheap drinks and an Elvis shrine lend an edge to the trendy scene here. It's good clean fun for hipster grandchildren of the beatniks. Regulars and visitors alike rave about the fried chicken.

6. Royale

N5 ⬛ 279 Tremont St ⬛ royale boston.com ⬛

A huge two-story dance hall, Royale occasionally morphs into a live-performance venue for touring acts.

7. Venu

N5 ⬛ 100 Warrenton St ⬛ Mon–Fri
⬛ venuboston.com

Music varies each weekend, but fashionable and glamorous visitors remain a constant. The Art Deco bar is a beautiful feature.

8. Jacque's Cabaret

N5 ⬛ 79 Broadway ⬛

A pioneer drag-queen bar, Jacque's features female impersonators, edgy rock bands, and cabaret shows.

9. The Beehive

M6 ⬛ 541 Tremont St ⬛ beehive boston.com

Live jazz, delicious cocktails and beers, and good, hearty fare make this one of the best venues in South End.

10. The Butcher Shop

F6 ⬛ 552 Tremont St

A full-service butcher shop and wine bar pairs sausages and salami with Italian, French, and Spanish wines by the glass or bottle. Gourmet "Burgers and Beers" evenings take place in the summer months.

Lauryn Hill performing at Royale

Asian Restaurants

1. Peach Farm
P5 24 Tyler St peachfarmseafood.com · $

Perfect for family-style dining, Peach Farm lets you select your choice of fish from a tank. Ask for the daily specials.

2. Pho Pasteur
P5 682 Washington St phopasteurboston.net · $

Refreshing Vietnamese noodle soups flavored with fresh herbs fill the menu here, but other Vietnamese dishes are also available.

3. Penang
P5 685 Washington St penangcuisineboston.com · $

Nominally "Pan-Asian," Penang has a chiefly Malay menu, ranging from inexpensive noodle staples to more contemporary concoctions.

4. Emperor's Garden
P5 690 Washington St (617) 482-8898 · $

Dim sum in this historical opera house is a theatrical experience. Note that most southern Chinese dishes are large and best shared.

5. Hei La Moon
P4 83 Essex St heilamoonrestaurant.com · $

A rather formal Pan-Chinese restaurant. On weekend mornings, a large crowd is guaranteed for the dim sum.

One of many tasty dishes at Peach Farm

Diners at Dumpling Café on Washington St

6. Taiwan Cafe
P5 34 Oxford St ordertaiwancafe.com · $

From its cafeteria appearance to its dishes like spicy big ears, this restaurant delivers one of the best regional Chinese dining experiences in the city.

7. Shojo
P5 9A Tyler St shojoboston.com · $

Savor suckling pig *bao* (steamed stuffed bun) and chicken tacos with *yuzu* slaw at this snazzy Japanese restaurant.

8. Dumpling King
P5 42 Beach St (617) 482-8888 Sat–Sun · $

This restaurant keeps it simple with a few tasty soups and dumplings filled with pork, leek, mushroom, or chicken.

9. Shabu-Zen
P5 16 Tyler St shabuzen.com · $$

Choose your meats, vegetables, and broth at this traditional Asian "hot-pot" joint.

10. Dumpling Café
P5 695 Washington St dumplingcafeboston.com · $

This casual spot sells several varieties of dumpling made fresh daily, alongside delicacies such as duck tongue.

Restaurants

1. B&G Oysters
F6 **550 Tremont St** **bandg oysters.com · $$$**
A seafood bistro acclaimed for its raw delicacies, B&G Oysters also has an excellent wine list.

2. Myers + Chang
G6 **145 Washington St** **myers andchang.com · $$**
Clever reinventions of classic Chinese dishes such as lemon shrimp dumplings are served here. Wash down with sake-based cocktails containing guava.

3. El Centro
F6 **472 Shawmut Ave** **elcentro inboston.com · $**
Delicious Mexican cuisine from a Sonoran chef that emphasizes fresh flavors. Expect excellent tamales and tortillas made from scratch.

4. Banyan Bar + Refuge
F6 **553 Tremont St** **banyan boston.com · $$**
A chic Pan-Asian gastropub, Banyan Bar + Refuge serves innovative fare such as roasted chicken with wasabi gratin potatoes and kimchi fried rice.

5. Troquet on South
Q5 **107 South St** **Sun & Mon** **troquetboston.com · $$$**
This American–French bistro recommends choosing your wine first and pairing your food order to its notes.

6. Toro
F6 **1704 Washington St** **L** **toro-restaurant.com · $$$**
Enjoy Barcelona-style tapas with Spanish wines and creative cocktails at this restaurant.

7. Aquitaine
F5 **569 Tremont St** **aquitaine boston.com · $$$**
A Parisian-style bistro popular for its snazzy wine bar and its French

market-style cooking. Black truffle vinaigrette makes Aquitaine's steak-frites Boston's best.

8. Franklin Cafe
F6 **278 Shawmut Ave** **L · $$**
Intimate South End favorite, serving American bistro fare along with creative cocktails, local beers, and affordable wines.

9. Ostra
N5 **1 Charles St S** **ostraboston. com · $$$**
This sophisticated restaurant in the Theater District serves contemporary Mediterranean fare in both innovative and classic dishes.

10. Petit Robert Bistro
L6 **480 Columbus Ave** **petit robertbistro.com · $$$**
Parisian chef Jacky Robert serves homey versions of classic French bistro food at lunch, dinner, and weekend brunch. There is also a great wine list.

Diners awaiting a table at El Centro

KENMORE AND THE FENWAY

On days when the Red Sox are playing a home baseball game at Fenway Park, Kenmore Square is packed with fans. By dusk, Kenmore becomes the jump-off point for a night of dancing, drinking, and socializing at clubs on or near Lansdowne Street. Yet for all of Kenmore's genial rowdiness, it is also the gateway into the sedate parkland of the Back Bay Fens and the stately late 19th- and early 20th-century buildings along the Fenway. Pedestrians can find Kenmore at night from miles away, thanks to its gigantic, animated Citgo sign serving as a somewhat surprising city landmark.

The Fenway neighborhood extends all the way southeast to Huntington Avenue; known as the "Avenue of the Arts," this tree-lined boulevard links key cultural centers such as Symphony Hall, Huntington Theatre, the Museum of Fine Arts, MassArt Art Museum, and the delightful and not-to-be-missed Isabella Stewart Gardner Museum.

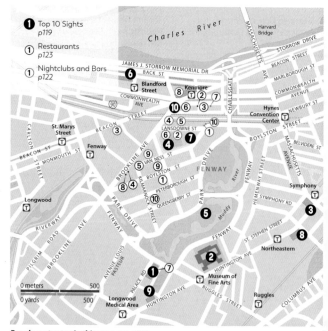

① Top 10 Sights
p119

① Restaurants
p123

① Nightclubs and Bars
p122

For places to stay in this area, see p150

Stained-glass window at the Isabella Stewart Gardner Museum

1 Isabella Stewart Gardner Museum

This Fenway museum *(p42)*, in a faux Venetian palace, represents the exquisite personal tastes of its founder, Isabella Stewart Gardner, who was one of the country's premier art collectors at the end of the 19th century.

2 Museum of Fine Arts

One of the largest fine arts museums in the country, the Museum of Fine Arts (MFA) *(p36)* is especially renowned for its collections of ancient Egyptian and Nubian art and artifacts, as well as of French Impressionism. Its Asian art holdings are said to be the largest in the US.

3 Symphony Hall

📍 E6 🏠 301 Massachusetts Ave
Ⓦ bso.org

The restrained, elegant Italian Renaissance exterior of this 1900 concert hall barely hints at what is considered to be the acoustic perfection of the interior hall. Home of the Boston Symphony Orchestra, the hall's 2,300-plus seats are usually sold out for classical concerts, as well as for the lighter Boston Pops.

4 Fenway Park

📍 D5 🏠 4 Jersey St Ⓦ redsox.com 🎫

Built in 1912, the home field of the Boston Red Sox is the oldest surviving park in major league baseball, and aficionados insist that it's also the finest. An odd-shaped parcel of land gives the park quirky features, such as the high, green-painted wall in left field, affectionately known as "the Green Monster." Tickets to games during the baseball season (April to October) can be hard to come by, but one-hour behind-the-scenes tours are offered throughout the year and include areas normally closed to the public, like the dugouts and private boxes.

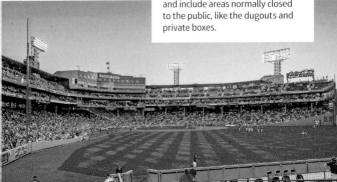

Fenway Park on game day

The verdant entrance to the Back Bay Fens

5 Back Bay Fens
D5–D6 **Bounded by Park Dr & the Fenway**

This lush ribbon of grassland, marshes, and stream banks follows Muddy River and forms one link in the Emerald Necklace of parks (p29). The enclosed James P. Kelleher Rose Garden in the center of the Fens offers a perfect spot for quiet contemplation. A path runs from Kenmore Square to the museums and galleries on Huntington Avenue, which makes a pleasant shortcut through the Fens. Best by daylight.

6 Boston University
C5 **Commonwealth Ave** **bu.edu**

Founded as a Methodist Seminary in 1839, Boston University was chartered as a university in 1869. Today it enrolls approximately 34,000 students from all 50 states and some 125 countries. The scattered colleges and schools were consolidated at the Charles River Campus in 1966. Both sides of Commonwealth Avenue are lined with distinctive university buildings and sculptures. The Howard Gotlieb Archival Research Center (771 Commonwealth Ave) lays emphasis on the memorabilia of show business figures, displayed on a rotating basis. Artifacts include Gene

Kelly's Oscar and a number of Bette Davis's film scripts. It also exhibits selections from its holdings of rare manuscripts and books. The Boston Playwrights' Theatre (949 Commonwealth Ave) was founded by the late Nobel Laureate Derek Walcott in 1981 to help develop new plays. A season highlight is the day-long Boston Theater Marathon of 50 ten-minute plays.

7 MGM Music Hall at Fenway
D5 **2 Lansdowne St** **crossroadspresents.com**

Located behind the right field bleachers of Fenway Park (p119), this state-of-the-art live performance venue stretches over four levels. While it accommodates more than 5,000 people, the hall's angled design and the placement of all seats, close to the center stage, creates an intimate feel for concertgoers.

8 Jordan Hall
E6 **30 Gainsborough St** **necmusic.edu**

This concert hall is in the New England Conservatory of Music (NEC). Musicians often praise its acoustics, heralding Jordan as "the Stradivarius of concert halls." Hundreds of free classical concerts are performed at this National Historic Landmark hall every year.

An orchestra performing in the magnificent Jordan Hall

9 MassArt Art Museum

ⓓ D6 ⓐ 621 Huntington Ave
ⓞ Noon-8pm Thu, noon-5pm Fri,
11am-5pm Sat & Sun ⓦ maam.
massart.edu

The MassArt Museum (set in the Massachusetts College of Art and Design's South Building) mounts some of Boston's most dynamic exhibitions of contemporary visual art. The school is the only independent state-supported art college in the US and exhibitions tend to emphasize avant-garde experimentation as well as social commentary and documentary.

10 Kenmore Square

ⓓ D5

Largely dominated by Boston University, Kenmore Square is now being transformed from a student area into an extension of upscale Back Bay. The square serves as the nexus of the B, C, and D branches of the MBTA's Green Line and is the public transportation gateway to Fenway Park. On game days, the square swarms with baseball fans and sidewalk vendors, rather than students. The most prominent landmark of the square is the Citgo sign, its more than 9,000 ft (2,743 m) of LEDs pulsing red, white, and blue from dusk until midnight. *Time* magazine designated this sign an "objet d'heart" because it was so beloved by Bostonians that they prevented its dismantling in 1983.

A DAY OF THE ARTS

Morning and afternoon

Take the Green Line "T" (B train) to Boston University Central and make your way to the **Howard Gotlieb Archival Research Center**, part of Boston University, for a glimpse of show business ephemera, such as Fred Astaire's dance shoes. Then head east toward **Kenmore Square** and cross over to Brookline Avenue. Make your way to **Fenway Park** (p119) for a tour of the stadium. Next, fill up on Mexican dishes at **El Pelón Taqueria** (p123) before wandering down Kilmarnock Street to reach **Back Bay Fens**, where you can rest beneath the wings of the angel on the Veterans Memorial. Continue to the **Museum of Fine Arts** (p36) to view the outstanding art collections. Afterward, follow the Fenway three blocks left to continue your immersion in art at the **Isabella Stewart Gardner Museum** (p42). Take a break in the "living room" of the museum's Renzo Piano-designed wing, then have a bite to eat at the classy **Café G** (p123).

Evening

You can pack in a full evening of entertainment by taking in a recital at **Jordan Hall**. When the final applause has died down, make your way to **Lucky Strike** (p122) and round off the night with billiards, bowling, and video games. You may want to continue into the early hours.

Nightclubs and Bars

1. Loretta's Last Call
D5 **1 Lansdowne St**
Country music and Southern food fuel this happening bar and dance club. The interior has a cozy, vintage vibe.

2. Bleacher Bar
D5 **82A Lansdowne St**
This tiny bar, tucked in the back of Fenway Park, has several seats offering direct views into the park.

3. Audubon Boston
D5 **838 Beacon St**
Close enough to Fenway Park to drop by after the game, Audubon Boston is a relaxed neighborhood bar and grill with good food, beer, and a thoughtful wine list.

4. Cask 'n Flagon
D5 **62 Brookline Ave**
At Fenway's premier sports bar, fans hoist a cold one and debate the merits of the Sox manager's latest tactics.

5. House of Blues
D5 **15 Lansdowne St** **house ofblues.com/boston**
An integral part of the nightlife scene around Fenway Park, the House of Blues hosts local as well as international bands and performers. A Gospel brunch is offered occasionally and the restaurant opens during Red Sox evening home games.

6. Game On!
D5 **82 Lansdowne St**
Wall-to-wall TVs are tuned to every game that's on anywhere in the country at this bar in a corner of Fenway Park. A prime spot for sports fans to eat, drink, and cheer.

7. The Kenmore
D5 **476 Commonwealth Ave**
Craft beers, burgers, hot dogs, and nachos make The Kenmore the perfect college hangout bar.

8. Cornwall's Pub
D5 **644 Beacon St**
As the name suggests, Cornwall's is a British-style pub with a wide range of good beers, ales, and food. Expect a relaxed atmosphere and crowds come game day.

9. Yard House
D5 **126 Brookline St**
Yard House offers more than 180 beers, from local brewers and beyond. It also serves excellent pub food – the menu features more than 100 items.

10. Lucky Strike
D5 **145 Ipswich St**
Set behind Fenway Park, this lively entertainment complex features bowling lanes, pool tables, and video games, plus the popular brewpub, Cheeky Monkey.

Live performance at the House of Blues

Restaurants

1. Citizen Public House
⚐ E5 **⌂** 1310 Boylston St **Ⓦ** citizenpub.com · $$
Craft beers, 100 whiskeys, excellent cocktails, and great pub food make Citizen a top neighborhood spot.

2. Eventide Fenway
⚐ D5 **⌂** 51321 Boylston St **Ⓦ** eventideoysterco.com/eventide-fenway · $$
Crowds congregate here to dine on freshly shucked oysters, brown butter lobster rolls, and whoopie pies.

3. India Quality
⚐ D5 **⌂** 484 Commonwealth Ave **Ⓦ** indiaquality.com · $
Long-time favorite of Boston University students, India Quality focuses on north Indian food roasted in a tandoor oven.

4. Sweet Cheeks Q
⚐ E5 **⌂** 1381 Boylston St **Ⓦ** sweetcheeksq.com ·$$
Chef-owner Tiffani Faison is all about Southern barbecue. Order pork belly by the pound and drink sweet tea.

5. Wahlburgers
⚐ D5 **⌂** 132 Brookline Ave **Ⓦ** wahlburgers.com · $
Chef Paul, brother of actor Mark Wahlberg, runs this casual restaurant, which serves burgers with a twist.

6. Tsurutontan Udon Noodle Brasserie
⚐ D5 **⌂** 512 Commonwealth Ave **Ⓦ** tsurutontan.com · $$
Udon noodle bowls and sushi may be the highlights of the menu at this place,

Simple interior of Sweet Cheeks Q, a popular hangout

but look out for indulgent Japanese treats such as creamy *uni* with caviar.

7. Café G
⚐ D6 **⌂** 25 Evans Way **Ⓦ** gardnermuseum.org/visit/cafe · $
Superb light fare, rich desserts, and fine wines at this spot complete a visit to the fabulous Isabella Stewart Gardner Museum (p42).

8. Nathálie Wine Bar
⚐ D5 **⌂** 186 Brookline Ave **Ⓒ** Sun & Mon **Ⓦ** nathaliebar.com · $$
Dishes such as flatiron steak, seared calamari, and bluefin crudo with aioli are accompanied by a great wine list here, which focuses on small-batch, natural wines that have been produced by women.

9. Tasty Burger
⚐ D5 **⌂** 86 Van Ness St **Ⓦ** tastyburger.com · $
This no-frills burger joint in the shadow of Fenway Park offers a variety of toppings and a wide assortment of beer. It's a good option for a pre-game bite before heading into the stadium.

10. El Pelón Taqueria
⚐ D5 **⌂** 92 Peterborough St **Ⓦ** elpelon.com · $
This charming little restaurant churns out tasty Mexican American treats at very competitive prices. Includes vegetarian and vegan dishes.

CAMBRIDGE AND SOMERVILLE

Harvard may be Cambridge's undeniable claim to worldwide fame, but that is not to diminish the city's vibrant neighborhoods, superb restaurants, unique shops, and busy bars lying just beyond the school's gates. Harvard Square, with its name-brand shopping and numerous coffeehouses, is a heady mix of urban bohemia and Main Street USA. To the northwest, the heavily residential city of Somerville has become a magnet for young artists, musicians, and social media influencers.

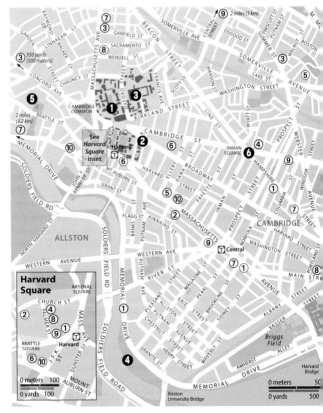

For places to stay in this area, see p150

1 Harvard University

While its stellar reputation might suggest visions of ivory towers in the sky, Harvard (p30) is a surprisingly accessible, welcoming place. Still, too often, visitors limit themselves to what is visible from the Yard: Massachusetts Hall, the Widener Library, maybe University Hall. But with other buildings by Gropius and Le Corbusier, top-notch museums, the eclectic Harvard Square, and performing arts spaces such as the Loeb Drama Center and Memorial Hall's Sanders Theatre lying just beyond the Yard, Harvard provides every incentive to linger a while.

2 Harvard Art Museums

B1 32 Quincy St 10am–5pm Tue–Sun harvardart museums.org

Harvard has some of the world's finest collegiate art collections. The Fogg, Sackler, and Busch-Reisinger museums, which make up the Harvard Art Museums, share space in a Renzo Piano-designed facility. Visitors will enjoy the surprising juxtapositions of Chinese bronzes, Greek vases, medieval altarpieces, and German Expressionist paintings.

3 Harvard Museums of Science & Culture

B1 9am–5pm daily peabody. harvard.edu; hmsc.harvard.edu

The Peabody Museum of Archaeology and Ethnology (11 Divinity Ave) excels at illustrating how interactions between distinct cultures influence people's lives. The Hall of the North American Indian displays artifacts reflecting the aftermath of encounters between Indigenous Americans and Europeans. The Museum of Natural History (26 Oxford St) has exhibits that display eons-old natural wonders. The botanical galleries include the Ware Collection of Blaschka Glass Models of Plants, known as the "glass flowers."

Davis Square

COLLEGE AVENUE
PEARL ST
FRANKLIN ST
STREET
Davis
MORRISON AVE
WILLOW AVE
9
6 8 2
HIGHLAND AVE
INGTON ST
RINDGE AVE
4
MASSACHUSETTS AVENUE
ORCHARD ST
ELM STREET
SUMMER STREET
10
Porter
2
SOMERVILLE AVENUE
3
Davis Square map area
Main map area
0 km 5
0 miles 5
0 meters 100
0 yards 100

CAMBRIDGE ST
OTIS ST
MONSIGNOR O'BRIAN HWY
THORNDIKE ST
SPRING ST
Lechmere
8
CHARLES ST
EAST CAMBRIDGE
6TH ST
10
BINNEY ST
3RD ST
2ND ST
1ST ST
EDWIN LAND BLVD
CAMBRIDGE PKWY
KENDALL SQUARE
BROADWAY
Kendall/MIT
AMHERST ST
MEMORIAL DRIVE
Charles River

A kachina doll on display at the Peabody Museum

4 Charles Riverbanks
⑨ B2–F3

Whether you're cheering the rowers of the Head of the Charles Regatta *(p60)* or watching the "T" cross Longfellow Bridge through a barrage of snow-flakes, the banks of the Charles River offer a fantastic vantage point for taking in Boston's celebrated scenes. On weekends from mid-April to November, the adjacent Memorial Drive becomes a sea of strollers, joggers, and rollerbladers.

5 Longfellow House
⑨ A1 ⓐ 105 Brattle St ⓒ For tours only; late May–Oct: 10am–4pm Fri–Mon ⓦ nps.gov/long ⓒ

Poet Henry Wadsworth Longfellow can be credited with helping to shape Boston's – and America's – collective identity. His poetic documentation of Paul Revere's midnight ride *(p24)* immortalized both him and his subject. In 1837, Longfellow took up residence in this house, a few blocks from Harvard Yard. He was not the first illustrious resident of this house. General George Washington headquartered and planned the 1776 siege of Boston in these rooms. The building is preserved with furnishings of Longfellow's family life, and houses the poet's archives.

6 Inman Square
⑨ D1

Often overlooked, Inman Square is possibly Cambridge's best-kept secret. Home to popular restaurants and cafés such as S&S Deli, 1369 Coffee House *(p129)*, and Trina's Starlight Lounge, plus Christina's delectable ice creams *(p71)*, Inman rewards those who are willing to go out of their way to experience a real-deal Cambridge neighborhood.

7 Massachusetts Institute of Technology (MIT)
⑨ E3 ⓐ 77 Massachusetts Ave ⓦ mit.edu ⓒ

MIT has been the country's leading technical university since its founding in 1861. Its List Visual Arts Center *(20 Ames St)* exhibits work that comments on technology or employs it in fresh, surprising ways. Also of note is the MIT Museum *(314 Main St)*, which blends art and science with exhibits such as artificial intelligence, Harold Edgerton's groundbreaking stroboscopic flash photographs, the latest holographic art, and the world's first computers.

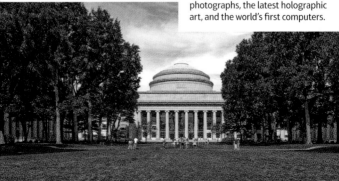

Performance at the Multicultural Arts Center

8 Multicultural Arts Center

F2 **41 2nd St** **10am–6pm Tue–Fri (to 8pm Thu)** **multiculturalartscenter.org**

The Multicultural Arts Center (MAC) presents a range of performances and visual art exhibitions which promote cross-cultural exchange, including summer programs in local parks. A unique feature is the encouragement of dialog between the audience and artists after performances.

9 Davis Square

With its cooler-than-thou coffee shops, lively bar scene, affordable restaurants, and the renowned Somerville Theatre, Davis Square, Somerville, stands as the area's most desirable neighborhood for many young Bostonians. And with prestigious Tufts University a 10-minute walk away, the square's youthful spirit is in a constant state of replenishment.

10 Museum of Science

The Museum of Science (MOS; p26) straddles the Charles River atop the inactive flood control dam that sits at its mouth. The MOS certainly knows how to make learning enjoyable – explore the cosmos in the Hayden Planetarium, admire a full-size model of a T-Rex, and experience larger-than-life IMAX® films in the Mugar Omni Theater. In addition to these attractions, the museum hosts blockbuster shows like Harry Potter: The Exhibit. Live presentations take place throughout the day.

Massachusetts Institute of Technology (MIT)

THE CAMBRIDGE CURRICULUM

Morning

Begin your morning with a cup of gourmet coffee and light breakfast at the popular **Diesel Café** (p64) on Davis Square. Next, ride the "T" inbound to Harvard and head straight to the independent **Harvard Book Store** (p72) to peruse its expertly curated selection of titles. Visit **Harvard Yard** (p30) and then walk east to Quincy Street and north to the **Harvard Art Museums** (p125). Walk south to Massachusetts Avenue, and turn right to legendary **Mr Bartley's** (1246 Massachusetts Ave) for lunch.

Afternoon

Ride the "T" inbound to **Kendall Square** and follow signage to the nearby **MIT Museum**, where exhibits of scientific, artistic, and technological innovations reflect the MIT's creative energy. Walk down Main Street to Central Square and ride the "T" to Park Street. Then ride the Green Line "T" to Science Park and the **Museum of Science**. In this museum you can view classic dioramas of New England. Then retrace your route on the "T" to Central Square, where you can enjoy a refreshing glass of orange wine on the patio at **Little Donkey** (505 Massachusetts Ave).

Offbeat Shops

Vintage comics on display at
The Million Year Picnic

1. Top Drawer
⬛ B1 ⬛ 5 Brattle St, Cambridge
From beautiful pens to Japanese
handkerchiefs, this is the perfect
place to pick up a gift.

2. Magpie
⬛ 416 Highland Ave, Somerville
This Davis Square boutique is packed
with handmade art and crafts by local
artists, goods from indie designers,
and "shiny things for your nest."

3. Ward Maps
⬛ 1731 Massachusetts Ave, Cambridge
In addition to some utterly lovely
antique map reproductions, this shop
stocks MBTA-themed items such as
mugs, key chains, and tote bags,
as well as toy trains and buses.

4. Motto
⬛ B1 ⬛ 26 Church St, Cambridge
A stylish shop selling women's
clothing, jewelry, and accessories
designed by up-and-coming names.
Motto also stocks stylish homeware,
including Japanese ceramics and
a range of greetings cards, with
striking designs.

5. Hubba Hubba
⬛ C2 ⬛ 2 Ellery St, Cambridge
If Cambridge's Puritanical founders
could see it now – spiked belts, accessories, leather corsets, and adult toys
line the shelves of this risqué boutique.

6. The Million Year Picnic
⬛ A1 ⬛ 99 Mt Auburn St, Cambridge
New England's oldest comic bookstore,
The Million Year Picnic keeps its faithful
customers happy with an extensive
back-issue selection, graphic novels,
rare imports, and all the latest indie
comics. Toys and T-shirts, too.

7. NOMAD
⬛ 1771 Massachusetts Ave, Cambridge
Clothing, folk art, and decor items from
around the globe are among the wares
for sale here. There is a visibly strong
emphasis on goods from Mexico and
Central America.

8. Davis Squared
⬛ 409 Highland Ave #2516, Somerville
This fun shop abounds with Davis
Square- and Somerville-themed
goods, ranging from coffee mugs
to wine decanters.

9. Cardullo's Gourmet Shoppe
⬛ B1 ⬛ 6 Brattle St, Cambridge
Harvard Square's oldest culinary
store specializes in gourmet foods
and beverages from around the
world. You can also buy made-to-
order deli sandwiches for lunch.

10. Mudflat Galley
⬛ 36 White St, Cambridge
Works by the artists and students
of Mudflat, a cooperative studio,
are on show at this gallery, found
in a glass arcade at the Porter Square
shopping center.

Places to Relax

1. Memorial Drive
🅰 A1–E3
Memorial Drive attracts joggers and rollerbladers. On weekends from mid-April to November, the road closes to vehicular traffic and becomes the city's best people-watching spot.

2. Porter Exchange
🅰 C2 🅰 1815 Massachusetts Ave, Cambridge
Many congregate at the food stalls in this Japanese-style noodle hall, housed in a handsome 1928 Art Deco building at Lesley University.

3. The Neighborhood
🅰 D1 🅰 25 Bow St, Somerville 🅦 theneighborhoodrestaurant.com · $
Enjoy Sunday brunch or Portuguese breakfast bread platters at this popular place.

4. 1369 Coffee House
🅰 D1 🅰 1369 Cambridge St, Cambridge 🅦 1369coffeehouse.com · $
Set on Inman Square, this branch of 1369 has poetry readings, mellow music, and courteous staff, which give it a neighborly atmosphere.

5. Brattle Theatre
🅰 B1 🅰 40 Brattle St, Cambridge 🅦 brattlefilm.org
A Harvard Square institution, the Brattle screens cinema greats daily.

Visiting on a rainy afternoon? Take in a 2-for-1 art house double feature for under $15.

6. Cambridge Public Library
🅰 C2 🅰 449 Broadway, Cambridge 🅦 cambridgepubliclibrary.org
Families with children, dog-owners tending to canine playgroups, and locals cover the lawns in warm weather. Indoors, folks stretch out in armchairs with a book and free Wi-Fi.

7. Fresh Pond Reservation
🅰 250 Fresh Pond Pkwy, Cambridge 🅦 cambridgema.gov
Join Cambridge's runners and dog-walkers on the 2.5-mile (4-km) loop trail around Fresh Pond. Along the way, look out for waterfowl and owls.

8. Club Passim
🅰 B1 🅰 47 Palmer St, Cambridge 🅦 passim.org
The subterranean epicenter of New England's thriving folk music scene regularly welcomes nationally renowned artists. It also has an on-site restaurant, The Kitchen, which serves dinner and Sunday brunch.

9. Trum Field
🅰 Broadway, Somerville
Summer in Somerville is epitomized by one thing – baseball at the playground. On most weeknights, you can watch energetic youngsters take their swings.

10. Dado Tea
🅰 C2 🅰 955 Massachusetts Ave, Cambridge 🅦 dadotea.com
This Massachusetts Avenue hangout, which is owned by locals, is a serene, tranquil place to settle in with a cup of tea. It's also an excellent place to enjoy some healthy pastries, sandwiches, wraps, and salads.

Enjoying some fresh air along Memorial Drive in Cambridge

Nightclubs and Bars

The Middle East live music club on Massachusetts Ave

1. The Middle East
📍 D3 🏠 472–480 Massachusetts Ave, Cambridge 🌐 mideastoffers.com ⏱
A live music club to rival any in New York or Los Angeles, the Middle East rocks its patrons from three stages and nourishes them with delicious kebabs and curries.

2. Sinclair
📍 B1 🏠 52 Church St
Harvard Square's primary live gig venue attracts a wide assortment of acts. The front room doubles as a trendy restaurant and lounge, and it's open into the small hours every night of the week.

3. Dear Annie
🏠 1741 Massachusetts Ave, Cambridge ⏱ Tue
This intimate bar serves an excellent array of fine and rare natural wines alongside locally sourced and homemade pescatarian dishes.

4. The Burren
🏠 247 Elm St, Somerville
🌐 burren.com
This friendly Irish bar features live music almost every night, and the performances range from Irish sessions to bluegrass to swing and jazz. The backroom has comedy, step-dancing, and a weekly open mic.

5. Backbar
📍 D1 🏠 7 Sanborn Ct, Somerville ⏱ Mon 🌐 bachbarunion.com
Somerville-Cambridge hipsters love this bar because of its gritty location, speakeasy vibe, and world-class cocktails. Learn to make your own by booking a cocktail class.

6. Hong Kong
📍 B2 🏠 238 Massachusetts Ave, Cambridge
Chinese food at ground level gives way to a bustling lounge on the second floor and a raucous comedy nightclub on the third. Tuesday night features a comic magic show.

7. Lord Hobo
📍 D2 🏠 92 Hampshire St, Cambridge
Forty draft beers, homey bistro food, and an inventive cocktail program draw an eclectic crowd, from hipsters to software geeks.

8. Lizard Lounge
📍 B1 🏠 1667 Massachusetts Ave, Cambridge
Just outside Harvard Square, the Lizard Lounge attracts a young, alternative rock- and folk-loving crowd with the promise of good live music and a small cover charge.

9. The Cantab Lounge
📍 C2 🏠 738 Massachusetts Ave, Cambridge
Live local rock performances, poetry slams, open mic nights, and other events light up the small but energetic stage at this blue-collar bar in Central Square.

10. Whitneys
📍 B2 🏠 37 John F. Kennedy St, Cambridge
This dive bar, located just south of Harvard Yard, was established in the 1950s. It offers classic American beers on draft and is also renowned for its hearty hot dogs.

Restaurants

PRICE CATEGORIES

For a three-course meal for one with half a bottle of wine (or equivalent meal), taxes, and extra charges.

$ under $40 **$$** $40–$60 **$$$** over $60

---

1. Oleana

📍 D2 🏠 134 Hampshire St, Cambridge 🕐 L 🌐 oleanarestaurant.com · **$$**

Chef Ana Sortun's mastery of spices is evident in Oleana's sumptuous Middle Eastern cuisine.

2. Pammy's

📍 C2 🏠 928 Massachusetts Ave, Cambridge 🕐 Sun 🌐 pammys cambridge.com · **$$$**

Flavors of New American cuisine are combined with Italian tradition to create delicious plates at Pammy's.

3. La Royal

🏠 221 Concord Ave, Cambridge 🌐 laroyalcambridge.com · **$$$**

Peru's regional dishes are showcased at this upscale spot, which has a changing weekly menu based on market produce.

4. Courthouse Seafood

📍 E2 🏠 498 Cambridge St, Cambridge 🕐 Sun & Mon 🌐 courthouseseafood. com · **$**

Adjoining a fish market, this no-frills restaurant is run by a Portuguese family. They always use the freshest catch in their food.

5. Catalyst

📍 E3 🏠 300 Technology Sq, Cambridge 🕐 Sun 🌐 catalystrestaurant.com · **$$$**

This elegant restaurant serves innovative locavore dishes. Craft beers attract the coders while good wines soothe the biotech execs.

6. Redbones

🏠 55 Chester St, Somerville 🕐 Mon 🌐 redbones.com · **$$**

Redbones creates some of the best barbecue north of the Carolinas, and the atmosphere is emphatically Southern.

7. Viale

📍 C3 🏠 502 Massachusetts Ave, Cambridge 🕐 L 🌐 vialecambridge. com · **$$$**

Delightful Mediterranean dishes and innovative cocktails make this friendly bar-restaurant a go-to place.

8. Area Four

📍 D3 🏠 500 Technology Sq, Cambridge 🌐 areafour.com · **$**

Service begins as early as 7am at this bakery-café, and continues into the night with New American comfort food and pizzas.

9. Puritan & Company

📍 D2 🏠 1166 Cambridge St, Cambridge 🕐 L Mon–Sat 🌐 puritancambridge. com · **$$$**

Excellent farm-to-table dining venue that re-invents New England cuisine with dishes such as seared scallops with tomatillos.

10. Harvest

📍 B1 🏠 44 Brattle St, Cambridge 🌐 harvestcambridge.com · **$$$**

This local institution serves delicious contemporary dishes prepared with fresh seasonal ingredients. The restaurant is known for its superb three-course Sunday brunch.

Grilled shrimp with *bucatini* at Pammy's

SOUTH OF BOSTON

South of Fort Point Channel, Boston's neighborhoods of Jamaica Plain (also known as "JP"), Roxbury, Dorchester, and South Boston are a mixture of densely residential streets and leafy parklands, the latter forming part of Frederick Law Olmsted's Emerald Necklace, a 7-mile (11-km) ring of parks. Often ignored by tourists, these areas make for a dynamic contrast to the homogenized city core, with quirky shops, countless restaurants, and a great mix of bars and nightclubs representing the many communities that make their homes here.

South Boston's defining characteristic has always been in relation to the harbor, and there is plenty to explore here, from long walks along a seaside promenade to climbing the steep hill to Dorchester Heights, with historic monuments and soft-sand beaches wedged in between. The 1-mile (1.5-km) Pleasure Bay Causeway is a favorite spot for joggers and speed walkers. While the areas south of Boston are a little harder to reach, it is well worth the effort to experience a more diverse Boston.

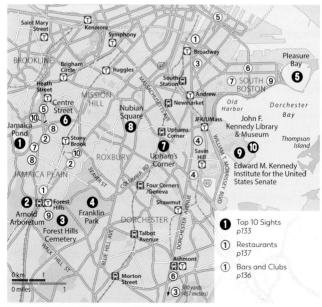

1	Top 10 Sights	p133
1	Restaurants	p137
1	Bars and Clubs	p136

For places to stay in this area, see p151

Glorious fall foliage at Jamaica Pond

1 Jamaica Pond

📍 Jamaica Pond Boathouse, Jamaica Way 🌐 boston.gov/parks/jamaica-pond

Offering an enchanting piece of countryside within the city, this pretty pond and its surrounding leafy park was landscaped by Frederick Law Olmsted to accentuate its natural glacial features. Locals enjoy the 1.5-mile (2.5-km) bankside path or fish in the 53-ft- (16-m-) deep glacial kettle pond (fishing requires a Massachusetts license; *call 617 626-1590*). While Jamaica Pond is open year-round, the boathouse rents small sailboats, kayaks, and rowboats in summer only.

2 Arnold Arboretum

📍 125 Arborway, Jamaica Plain 🌐 arboretum.harvard.edu

One of the US's foremost collections of temperate-zone trees and shrubs covers the peaceful 0.4-sq-mile- (1.1-sq-km-) arboretum. Grouped in scientific fashion, they are a favorite subject for landscape painters, and a popular resource for botanists and gardeners. The world's most extensive lilac collection blooms from early May through late June, and thousands of Bostonians turn out for Lilac Sunday, on the second Sunday in May, to picnic and enjoy the peak of the Syringa blooms. The main flowering period of mountain laurel, azaleas, and other rhododendrons begins around Memorial Day (at the end of May).

3 Forest Hills Cemetery

📍 95 Forest Hills Ave, Jamaica Plain 🌐 foresthillscemetery.com

More than 100,000 graves dot the rolling landscape in this Victorian "garden cemetery," one of the first of its kind. Maps available at the entrance identify the graves of notable figures, such as poet E. E. Cummings and playwright Eugene O'Neill. Striking memorials include the bas-relief *Death Stays the Hand of the Artist* by Daniel Chester French, near the main entrance.

4 Franklin Park

📍 Franklin Park Rd, Dorchester 🌐 boston.gov/parks/franklin-park

Frederick Law Olmsted considered Franklin Park the masterpiece of his Emerald Necklace (*p29*), but his vision of urban wilds has since been modified to more modern uses. The park is home to the second-oldest municipal golf course in the US, as well as vast swaths of oak forest that teem with native New England wildlife, such as turkeys, deer, and squirrels.

Franklin Park covered in snow on a bright winter's day

Kiteboarding on calm waters at Pleasure Bay

5 Pleasure Bay

South Boston's Pleasure Bay park encloses a pond-like cove of Boston Harbor with a causeway boardwalk, where locals turn out for their daily constitutionals. Halfway along is the Head Island light pavilion, with picnic tables. Castle Island (p52), now attached to the mainland, has guarded the mouth of Boston Harbor since the first fortress was erected in 1634. As New England's oldest continually fortified site, it is now guarded by Fort Independence (c. 1851). Anglers gather on the adjacent Steel Pier and drop bait into the mass of striped bass and bluefish.

6 Centre Street

Jamaica Plain is home to many artists, musicians, and writers as well as a substantial portion of Boston's LGBTQ+ community. Centre Street is the main artery and neighborhood hub. There is a distinctly Latin American flavor at the Jackson Square end, where Caribbean music shops and Cuban, Dominican, and Mexican restaurants abound. At the 600 block, Centre Street morphs into an urban countercultural village, with design boutiques, funky secondhand stores, and small cafés and restaurants.

7 Upham's Corner

🏛 Strand Theatre, 543 Columbia Rd, Dorchester 📞 (617) 635-1403

The area known as Upham's Corner was founded in 1630, and its venerable Old Dorchester Burial Ground contains ethereal carved stones from this Puritan era. Today, Upham's Corner is decidedly more Caribbean than Puritan, with shops specializing in food, clothing, and the music of the islands. The Strand Theatre, a 1918 luxury movie palace and vaudeville hall, functions as an arts center and venue for live concerts and other community events.

8 Nubian Square

Roxbury's Nubian Square is the heart of African American Boston as well as the busiest hub in the city's public transportation network. A few blocks from the square, the modest Georgian-style Dillaway-Thomas House (183 Roxbury St) reveals Roxbury's early history, including the period when it served as headquarters for the Continental Army's General John Thomas during the Siege of Boston. Exhibits at the house reflect the area's

Exterior of the John F. Kennedy Library and Museum

history from the colonial era to the present as a center of African American culture in Boston.

9 Edward M. Kennedy Institute for the United States Senate

🏠 210 Morrissey Blvd, Dorchester
🕐 By appointment, chech website
🌐 emkinstitute.org 🗗

Displaying re-creations of the US Senate Chamber and Senator Edward M. Kennedy's office, this facility provides an impressive interactive experience of how the Senate functions. With film and live actors, "Great Senate Debates" re-creates historic turning points.

10 John F. Kennedy Library and Museum

🏠 Columbia Point, Dorchester
🕐 10am–5pm daily 🌐 jfklibrary.org 🗗

This nine-story pyramidal building designed by I. M. Pei in 1977 stands like a billowing sail on Columbia Point, near the mouth of Boston Harbor. Inside the soaring white concrete-and-glass building, exhibits recount the 1,000 days of the Kennedy presidency. Kennedy was the first president to grasp the power of broadcast, and video exhibits include campaign debates, as well as coverage of his assassination and funeral.

STREET HEAT & POND COOL IN JAMAICA PLAIN

Afternoon

The Orange Line "T" delivers you to the Latin American end of Jamaica Plain's **Centre Street** at **Jackson Square**. Head west to enjoy empanadas, coffee, and Latin American desserts at **Gondres Bakery** (333 Centre St). A walk along Centre Street serves a cornucopia of Latin American fashion and specialty shops. Follow Centre Street as it doglegs left. Hip **Streetcar** (488 Centre St) carries a large selection of boutique wines and craft beers. At **J P Licks** (659 Centre St) order a cone of super-premium ice cream. **Kitchenwitch** (671 Centre St) features all kinds of kitchenware, including bamboo salt boxes and silicon handles for cast-iron skillets. Jeweler Phil Celeste carries unique clothing, jewelry, and gift items at **On Centre** (676 Centre St). The thrift store **Boomerangs** (716 Centre St) has clothing and home decor. **Salmagundi** (765 Centre St) is the place to go for hat shopping. Wander up Burroughs Street and cross Jamaica Way to **Jamaica Pond** (p133) to stroll, sit in the shade, or rent a rowboat.

Evening

Work up an appetite and return to Centre Street for dinner at **Vee Vee** (p137). Afterward, hit ultra-hip **Midway Cafe** (p136) for a chilled beer and live music.

Bars and Clubs

1. The Jeanie Johnston
📍 144 South St, Jamaica Plain
This entertainment venue has plenty to offer, with an open mic on Thursdays, live local bands on Fridays, and karaoke on Saturdays. There's a snug spot to sit with one of its 35 draft beers.

2. Midway Cafe
📍 3496 Washington St, Jamaica Plain
A fixture on the Boston live music scene since 1987, Midway hosts every kind of band imaginable. The highlight of the weekly calendar is Thursday night's "Queeraoke."

3. Castle Island Brewing Co.
📍 10 Old Colony Rd, South Boston
This 10-barrel brewery tasting room serves award-winning beers and South Shore-style pizza. Expect regular events, including live music most Friday nights.

4. dbar
📍 1236 Dorchester Ave, Dorchester
🕙 Mon
Dbar's eclectic dinner menu disappears around 10pm, when it morphs into a diverse nightclub where brightly colored cocktails are a specialty. Enjoy show tunes on Tuesdays, and karaoke on Fridays.

5. Lucky's Lounge
📍 355 Congress St, South Boston
A Fort Point Channel underground bar that swaggers with rat-pack retro ambience, right down to the unmissable Frank Sinatra tribute nights.

6. The Broadway
📍 726 East Broadway, South Boston
On weekends this watering hole is packed both inside and outside in the garden. Modern pub food hits a fairly high mark.

7. L Street Tavern
📍 658A East 8th St, South Boston
One of Southie's most old-fashioned pubs, L Street serves Harpoon and Guinness on tap. The Oscar-winning movie *Good Will Hunting* was filmed here.

8. Brendan Behan Pub
📍 378 Centre St, Jamaica Plain
This Irish pub is named after the Irish playwright Brendan Behan. Visit for a pint of beer and live music, and stay for the charming ambience.

9. Local 149
📍 149 P St, South Boston
This neighborhood joint has local beers on tap, creative cocktails, and some of the best New American food outside of a fancy restaurant.

10. The Haven
📍 284 Amory, Jamaica Plain
One of the city's most active purveyors of Scottish craft beers, ales, and ciders, the Haven also features an extensive single malt whisky collection. Do not miss the fine lamb haggis.

A crowd forming at Midway Cafe

Restaurants

Dining at the Yellow Door Taqueria in the South End of Boston

1. Fox & the Knife

📍 28 W Broadway, South Boston
🌐 foxandtheknife.com · $$

Inspired by the chef's stay in Modena, Italy, this chic little enoteca serves locally focused Italian cuisine in a laid-back space. The handmade pasta is heavenly.

2. Tres Gatos

📍 470 Centre St, Jamaica Plain
🌐 tresgatosjp.com · $$

This part tapas bar, part book and music store features typical Spanish bar dishes along with some inventive variants.

3. Yellow Door Taqueria

📍 2297 Dorchester Ave 🕐 L 🌐 yellow doortaqueria.com · $

Specializing in craft cocktails, rare tequila, and local beer, this snazzy Mexican bar serves innovative tacos, healthy salads, and great ceviches.

4. Ba Le Restaurant

📍 1052 Dorchester Ave, Dorchester
🌐 balebanhmiboston.com · $$

A testament to Dorchester's thriving Vietnamese dining scene, this venue is a top spot for Southeast Asian dishes.

5. Miami Restaurant

📍 381 Centre St, Jamaica Plain
🌐 ordermiamirestaurant.com · $

This place is the self-proclaimed "King of the Cuban sandwiches." Check out the photos of the Latin American pro baseball players who often eat here when they're in town.

6. Tavolo Dot Ave

📍 1918 Dorchester Ave, Dorchester
🕐 Mon 🌐 tavolodotave.com · $$

An Ashmont neighborhood staple, Tavolo serves market-fresh and rustic Italian dishes.

7. Ten Tables

📍 597 Centre St, Jamaica Plain
🕐 Mon & Tue 🌐 tentables.net · $$$

A small venue with just ten tables, this restaurant has an equally compact but rewarding menu, such as scallops on minted pea tendrils.

8. Vee Vee

📍 763 Centre St, Jamaica Plain
🕐 Sun & Mon 🌐 veeveejp.square space.com · $$$

Delectable American bistro fare makes this restaurant a favorite with local foodies, especially since many dishes have vegetarian versions. The Sunday brunch is very popular.

9. Brassica Kitchen + Cafe

📍 3710 Washingon St, Jamaica Plain
🕐 Mon & Tue 🌐 brassicakitchen.com · $$

Rumor has it that Brassica serves Boston's best fried chicken. Order and decide for yourself. Expect a pastry-centric menu if you are visiting at breakfast or brunch time.

10. Blue Nile

📍 389 Centre St, Jamaica Plain
🕐 Mon 🌐 bluenileincjp.com · $

Vegetables take center stage in the Ethiopian home-style dishes served here, but there are also plenty of meat and fish options.

STREETSMART

Boston's North Station

GETTING AROUND

Whether you're exploring Boston on foot or making use of public transportation, here is everything you need to know to navigate the city and surrounding region like a pro.

Arriving by Air

Logan International Airport (BOS) is located 2 miles (3 km) northeast of downtown Boston. Transportation to central Boston is accessed from the baggage claim area. Free buses link terminals to the Blue Line subway and South Station (via the free MBTA Silver Line bus). Taxis wait at all terminals but airport fees can make rides expensive. Logan Airport is also served by ride-sharing companies. Shuttle services are available via **Massport** to locations in downtown Boston and to eastern Massachusetts.

For the scenic water route, take a water taxi, operated by **Boston Water Taxi** or **Rowes Wharf Water Transport**, to Logan Dock. The free Route 66 airport water shuttle connects the dock to other areas of the airport.

Several international and some domestic charters use **Manchester Airport** (MHT) in New Hampshire, 50 miles (79 km) from Boston, and **T. F. Green Airport** (PVD), near Providence, Rhode Island, 59 miles (95 km) from Boston. Buses to Boston run from both.

Boston Water Taxi
W bostonharborcruises.com
Logan International Airport
W massport.com
Manchester Airport
W flymanchester.com
Massport
W massport.com
Rowes Wharf Water Transport
W roweswharfwatertransport.com
T. F. Green Airport
W flyri.com

Domestic Train Travel

Amtrak intercity rail services arrive into Boston at South Station from various other cities in the US. Rail services from New York take three to five hours and are very frequent.

Amtrak also connects Boston with the rest of New England. The Northeast Regional route, which departs from

South Station, connects the city to Long Island Sound, Connecticut, and Providence. Amtrak's daily Downeaster service leaves Boston's North Station, with stops in New Hampshire, and ends in Brunswick, Maine.

Amtrak
🆆 amtrak.com

Long-Distance Bus Travel

Most intercity coaches to Boston use South Station Transportation Center, the city's primary bus station, which is part of Amtrak and the MBTA subway system. **Greyhound** offers routes between Boston and many US cities. Other lines include **Megabus**, **Flixbus**, and **Peter Pan**.

Flixbus
🆆 flixbus.com
Greyhound
🆆 greyhound.com
Megabus
🆆 megabus.com
Peter Pan
🆆 peterpanbus.com

Public Transportation

The Massachusetts Bay Transportation Authority (**MBTA**) operates the subway (known more commonly as the "T"), bus lines, and some ferry services in the Metropolitan Boston area as well as commuter rail options stretching north to Newburyport, Massachusetts, west to Worcester, and south to Providence, Rhode Island. Safety and hygiene measures, timetables, ticket information, transportation maps, and more can be obtained from the MBTA website.

MBTA
🆆 mbta.com

Tickets

Fares and ticket options for the MBTA network vary depending on the form of transportation. There are four ways to purchase a ticket: with cash, the electronic mTicket app, a plastic CharlieCard, or a paper CharlieTicket.

Use cash to buy bus, subway, trolley, ferry, and commuter rail tickets via the onboard fare boxes or street-level stops.

Android and iPhone users can download the mTicket app, and use it to purchase tickets and passes for ferries and commuter rail lines.

Intended largely for residents, CharlieCards are only valid on the city's buses, subway, and Silver Line.

CharlieTickets can be purchased at any MBTA vending machine and loaded with a single trip ($2.40 subway/$1.70 bus), a 24-hour pass ($11), or 7-day pass ($22.50). CharlieTickets that are loaded with a single trip are only valid on buses, the subway, and the Silver Line, while those loaded with a pass can be used throughout Boston's public transportation system. This is the best option for visitors planning on traveling around the city.

GETTING TO AND FROM THE AIRPORT

Airport	Transportation	Journey Time	Price
Logan International Airport	Taxi	15 mins	$35-40
	Shuttle	30-45 mins	$3-9
	MBTA Silver Line	15-25 mins	Arriving free; departing $2.40
	Water Taxi	10-12 mins	$20
Manchester Airport	Taxi	1 hr	$70-90
	Bus	1 hr	$10-20
T. F. Green Airport	Taxi	1 hr 20 mins	$80-100
	Bus	$25-35	1 hour

Subway

Boston's combined subway and trolley network, known as the "T", is run by the MBTA. It usually operates 5am–1am daily (from 6am on Sundays). Weekday service is every 3–15 minutes; note that it is less frequent on weekends. There are five lines: Red, from south of the city to Cambridge; Green, from Somerville and Medford westward to Brookline, Newton, and Jamaica Plain; Blue, from near Government Center to Logan International Airport and on to Revere; Orange, linking the northern suburbs to Forest Hills in Roxbury; and Silver, a surface bus that runs from Roxbury to Logan International Airport via South Station.

Maps of Boston's subway system are available at Downtown Crossing MBTA station, or online.

Bus

The MBTA bus system covers most of the city. Two useful sightseeing routes are No. 93 Haymarket–Charlestown (from near Quincy Market to Bunker Hill) and No. 1 Harvard–Nubian (from Harvard Square via Massachusetts Avenue to Back Bay and continuing to Nubian Square in Roxbury via South End). The Silver Line, which provides quick trips to airport or cruise ship terminals, is also convenient. Maps are available on the MBTA website or at the office at Downtown Crossing. Alternatively, download the YourBus MBTA app to track arrivals at any given stop.

Taxis

Due to the popularity of Lyft and Uber ride-hailing services, taxicabs are becoming increasingly scarce, though cabs can still be hired at the airport, outside major hotels, on the street in the downtown area or at taxi stands.

Note that cab companies that operate in the Boston Metropolitan area are limited to picking up in the cities where they are chartered. A Boston cab cannot pick up in Cambridge or vice versa.

Driving

Boston's public transportation system makes it easy to be without a car. Nonetheless, driving is the most convenient way to explore beyond the city.

Driving to Boston

The I-95 superhighway (also known as Route 128) is the main entry to New England from New York and points south. This major highway runs close to the coast through Connecticut and Rhode Island to the outskirts of Boston. Here, it connects with roads into the city.

The I-90, also known as the Massachusetts Turnpike, is the main route into the city from the west.

From the north, the I-89 starts in northwestern Vermont, then cuts diagonally from Burlington to Concord, New Hampshire, where it links up with I-93 into Boston. The I-93 enters Boston from the north over the Zakim bridge. It crosses the city north to south as an underground expressway, known as the Thomas P. "Tip" O'Neill Jr. Tunnel. Watch signs carefully for exits.

Driving in Boston

Driving in the city can be stressful. The narrow streets are laid out in a confusing manner with little signage. There are few gas stations, limited parking with time-of-day restrictions, and many one-way streets and traffic circles.

If you do decide to travel by car in Boston, and are unfamiliar with the city, an up-to-date GPS and advance planning are essential for ensuring a stress-free experience.

Parking lots are very expensive in the city center. It is cheaper to park on-street. Note, however, that on-street parking meters have a two-hour limit, residents-only rules are strictly enforced, and fines are high.

It is far easier to drive outside the city. Divided highways connect Boston to New England's other major cities. Rural New England rewards road trippers, especially during fall foliage season, when the region's roads are fringed by golden, red, and orange leaves. Summer is also a great time to hit the road, although heavy traffic can slow progress on popular roads during peak season. Driving in winter and early spring has its challenges. Snow and ice call for special driving skills, and frost heaves create sidewalk cracks and potholes.

Car Rental
To rent a car in Boston you must be at least 21 years old, and have a valid credit card. Some rental companies charge an extra fee to drivers under the age of 25. Major international car rental agencies have outlets at Logan Airport, as well as elsewhere in the city. Collision damage waiver and liability insurances are often not included but are highly recommended.

Rules of the Road
Third-party insurance is required and you should always carry your policy documents and driving license.

Drive on the right. Pass only on the outside or left-hand lane, and when approaching a traffic circle, give priority to traffic already on the circle.

Seat belts must be worn at all times by the driver and passengers. Young children should be in child seats buckled into the back seat. Use of a handheld device (like a mobile phone) while driving is against the law.

Cycling
Compared to many US cities, Boston has an excellent cycling infrastructure. Bike-sharing scheme **Bluebikes** operates at stations throughout Boston and Cambridge. Central Boston and Cambridge have many bike lanes along major city streets, including Dutch-style protected lanes. Otherwise, it is legal to pedal on city streets, though cycling on highways is illegal. Riding on sidewalks is permitted only when moving at a walking pace, and you should always give way to pedestrians.

Boston also offers a surprising number of opportunities for off-road cycling. A designated bike path runs through the verdant **Southwest Corridor Park** and a circular, cycling-friendly loop takes in the **Emerald Necklace** chain of parks. There are also paths around the Charles River basin between the Charles River Dam and Watertown. If you're traveling with kids, a good option is the **Minuteman Bikeway**, a paved bike path on a former rail line which links Cambridge, Arlington, Lexington, Concord, and Bedford. As no vehicles are allowed to travel along the bikeway, it is safe for even the most unsteady of cyclists.

Helmets and high-visibility clothing are not obligatory for adults, but wearing them is strongly advised. Riders aged 16 and younger must wear helmets.

Bluebikes
🌐 bluebikes.com
Emerald Necklace
🌐 emeraldnecklace.org
Minuteman Bikeway
🌐 minutemanbikeway.org
Southwest Corridor Park
🌐 swcpc.org/bicycling.asp

Walking and Hiking
Downtown Boston is compact and easy to get around on foot. Stay on sidewalks and cross only at marked intersections. Several companies run walking tours and there are even routes for particular interests like movies or food.

For a very urbanized city, Boston also has some excellent hiking trails. Chief among them is the 43-mile (69-km) waterfront path known as the **Boston Harborwalk**. It stretches from the Neponset River to Belle Isle Marsh. Another excellent walking destination is the Arnold Arboretum (p133). This preserve is crisscrossed with walking trails and is especially striking during the fall foliage season, when the trees put on one of nature's greatest shows.

Boston Harborwalk
🌐 bostonharbornow.org

PRACTICAL INFORMATION

A little local know-how goes a long way in Boston. On these pages you can find all the essential advice and information you will need to make the most of your trip to this city.

AT A GLANCE

CURRENCY
US Dollar

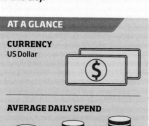

AVERAGE DAILY SPEND

SAVE	SPEND	SPLURGE
$120	$200	$300+

BOTTLED WATER	COFFEE	BEER	DINNER FOR TWO
$2-$3	$3-$5	$8-$12	$120

CLIMATE

The longest days occur May through September, while November through February has the shortest.

Average temperatures range from 73°F (23°C) in summer to 25°F (-4°C) in winter.

October through December sees the most rainfall. Expect snowfall December through February.

ELECTRICITY SUPPLY
The standard electric current is 110 volts and 60 Hz. Power sockets are type A and B, fitting plugs with two flat pins.

Passports and Visas
For entry requirements, including visas, consult your nearest US embassy or check with the **US Department of State**. All travelers to the US need a passport that is valid for six months longer than their intended period of stay. Canadian visitors only require a valid passport. Citizens of the UK, Australia, New Zealand, and the EU do not need a visa, but must apply in advance for the Electronic System for Travel Authorization (**ESTA**). All other visitors will require a visa.
ESTA
w esta.cbp.dhs.gov/esta
US Department of State
w travel.state.gov

Government Advice
Now more than ever, it is important to consult both your and the US government's advice before traveling. The US Department of State, the UK Foreign, Commonwealth and Development Office (**FCDO**), and the **Australian Department of Foreign Affairs and Trade** offer the latest information on security, health, and local regulations.
Australian Department of Foreign Affairs and Trade
w smartraveller.gov.au
FCDO
w gov.uk/foreign-travel-advice

Customs Information
You can find information on the laws relating to goods and currency taken in or out of the US on the **Customs and Border Protection Agency** website.
Customs and Border Protection Agency
w cbp.gov/travel

Insurance
We recommend that you take out a comprehensive insurance policy covering theft, loss of belongings, medical care, cancelations, and delays, and read the small print carefully. All

medical treatment is private and US health insurers do not have reciprocal arrangements, so it is important to take out medical insurance.

Vaccinations

No inoculations are required for visiting the US.

Money

Most establishments accept major credit, debit, and prepaid currency cards. Contactless payments are preferred; however, it is always worth carrying some cash for smaller items and tips. Cash machines can be found at banks, stations, and on main streets.

Tipping is customary. In restaurants, tip 15 to 20 percent of the total bill. Hotel porters and housekeeping expect $1 per bag or day, and you should round up taxi fares to the nearest dollar.

Travelers with Specific Requirements

The **Society for Accessible Travel and Hospitality** and **Mobility International** offer information for people with disabilities.

All facilities renovated or newly built since 1987 are legally required to provide wheelchair-accessible entrances and restrooms. Government buildings, museums, and theaters are accessible, but call ahead to verify that tours can meet your needs. It is best to call historic buildings, hotels, and restaurants in advance to ask about amenities. The website of the **Greater Boston Convention & Visitors Bureau** has access information and contact numbers for a range of places and tours.

All establishments allow service animals, and most busy road intersections have audio signals for safe crossing times.

Most MBTA commuter rail lines, buses, subways, and ferries accommodate wheelchairs; check the MBTA website (p141) for details. Logan International Airport (p140) has accessible ramps, elevators, and restrooms, plus a list of accessible transportation to and from the airport on its website.

Greater Boston Convention & Visitors Bureau
W bostonusa.com/plan/transport ation/getting-around/accessibility
Mobility International
W miusa.org
Society for Accessible Travel and Hospitality
W sath.org

Language

English is the principal language spoken in Boston, although you might hear Spanish, Italian, Mandarin, and Cantonese around the city.

Opening Hours

Museums are usually open 10am (noon on Sun) to 5pm and some are closed on Mondays.

Stores open at 10am or 11am and close at 6pm or 7pm Monday to Saturday, while on Sunday many shops open late and close early.

Most banks are open 9am to 4pm or 5pm Monday to Friday, and some also open on Saturday morning.

On Federal and State holidays most places close early or for the day.

In winter, some attractions close weekdays from mid-October to the end of December, and a few close entirely January through March.

MBTA trains begin at about 5am Monday to Saturday, 6am on Sunday, and end between midnight and 1am every night. Each line and each station varies so check ahead.

Situations can change quickly and unexpectedly. Always check before visiting attractions and hospitality venues for up-to-date opening hours and booking requirements.

Personal Security

Boston is generally safe but petty crime does take place. Pickpockets work known tourist areas and busy streets. Use your common sense, keep valuables in a safe place, and be alert to your surroundings. Lock your car and always store valuables in the trunk.

AT A GLANCE

EMERGENCY NUMBERS

GENERAL
EMERGENCY

911

TIME ZONE
EST/EDT
Eastern Daylight Time
(EDT) is observed
Mar 9–Nov 2, 2025;
Mar 8–Nov 1, 2026;
Mar 14–Nov 7, 2027.

TAP WATER
Unless otherwise stated, tap water is safe to drink.

WEBSITES AND APPS

meetboston.com
Greater Boston's official tourist information site.

NECN.com
The regional cable news company's website offers real-time traffic updates.

nws.com
The National Weather Service offers detailed weather information.

visitcambridge.org
Cambridge's official tourist information website.

visitnewengland.com
New England's official tourist board website for overseas visitors.

If you have anything stolen, report the crime as soon as possible to the **Boston Police Department**. Get a copy of the crime report to claim on your insurance. Within the MBTA's service area, you can also ask the **MBTA Transit Police** for help. Contact your embassy or consulate immediately if your passport is stolen or in the event of a serious crime or accident.

As a rule, Bostonians are very accepting of all people, regardless of their race, gender, or sexuality. The country's abolitionist and women's suffrage movements both started here, and Massachusetts was the first US state to legalize same-sex marriage (in 2003). Today, Boston has the largest LGBTQ+ population in the region. If you do feel unsafe, the **Safe Space Alliance** pinpoints your nearest place of refuge.

Boston Police Department
📞 (617) 343-4500
MBTA Transit Police
📞 (617) 222-1212
Safe Space Alliance
🌐 safespacealliance.com

Health

The US does not have a government health program, so emergency medical and dental care, though excellent, can be very expensive. Medical travel insurance is highly recommended in order to cover some of the costs related to an accident or sudden illness. The price of basic care at a hospital emergency room can rise incredibly quickly. Should you be in a serious accident, an ambulance will pick up and charge later.

If you need a prescription dispensed, there are pharmacies (drugstores) that stay open 24 hours. Ask your hotel for the nearest one.

Smoking, Alcohol, and Drugs

Smoking and "vaping" are banned in all public spaces such as bus and train stations, airports, and in enclosed areas of bars, cafés, restaurants, and hotels. However, many bars and restaurants have outdoor areas where smoking is permitted.

Alcohol may not be sold to or bought for anyone under the age of 21. The legal blood alcohol limit for drivers is 0.08 percent. Avoid drinking alcohol if you plan to drive.

Recreational cannabis use by adults is fully legal in Massachusetts, but public consumption is discouraged. Purchases may be made by adults at licensed cannabis dispensaries. Do not carry drugs purchased in Massachusetts on airplanes, as federal law is far less permissive. There is no objective standard of impairment if a driver has been using cannabis, but operating a vehicle while under the influence is a crime.

ID
Passports are required as ID at airports. (American citizens may use a state driver's license to board domestic flights.) Anyone who looks under 25 may be asked for photo ID to prove their age when buying alcohol, tobacco, or cannabis products.

Responsible Travel
New England is one of the US's most environmentally conscious regions. Forty percent of the region's energy is from renewable sources, and Boston is recognized by the Natural Resources Defense Council as the greenest city on the East Coast. Visitors find it easier than ever to be environmentally aware here. Recycling facilities are common, and community farmers' markets selling local produce and artisan foodstuffs can be found almost everywhere.

Cell Phones and Wi-Fi
Free Wi-Fi hot spots are widely available in Boston and Cambridge. Almost all hotels, motels, and inns offer free Wi-Fi, as do many cafés, bars, restaurants, and even some public parks.

Visitors from outside the US can buy pay-as-you-go SIM cards for GSM phones at airports and most phone stores. Some networks also sell basic flip phones (with minutes) for as little as $25 (no paperwork or ID required). Canadian residents can usually upgrade their domestic cell phone plan to extend to the US. Pre-paid phone cards usually offer the best rates for international calls, and are sold in many drugstores and convenience markets.

Postal Services
Boston and Cambridge have several offices of the US Postal Service. Post offices are open at least 9am–5pm weekdays, with some branches open on Saturdays. The branch near South Station is open daily 6am–midnight. All others are closed on Sundays. Letters and small parcels (less than 13 oz/370 g) with correct postage can be placed in any blue mailbox.

Taxes and Refunds
It is important to remember that listed prices rarely include applicable taxes. Massachusetts sales tax of 6.25 percent is levied on all items except non-restaurant food and clothing under $175. State meal tax is also 6.25 percent. Lodging tax in Boston and Cambridge is 8.45 percent in addition to the state sales tax. Because these taxes are not levied at a national level, international visitors cannot claim refunds.

Discount Cards
Many of Boston's museums, galleries, and attractions offer discounts to students and senior citizens. A valid form of ID is required. Students from abroad should carry an International Student Identity Card (**ISIC**) to claim discounts on hostel accommodations, museums, and theaters. Over-50s should look into buying an **AARP** membership (open to non-Americans), which can provide discounts at hotels and on car rentals.

AARP
W aarp.org
ISIC
W isic.org

PLACES TO STAY

Boston's accommodations range from beautiful
Art Nouveau hotels to homely B&Bs. The best area
to stay really depends on the experience you want:
Beacon Hill has options conveniently located to
historical sites while downtown Boston is ideal
for those who want a quiet night, for example.

Take the opportunity to stay in one of Boston's
historic buildings. Spend the night in a former
Victorian firehouse or 19th-century jail, or check
into an inn that pioneered the Boston cream pie.

> **PRICE CATEGORIES**
> For a standard, double
> room per night (with
> breakfast if included),
> taxes, and extra charges.
>
> **$** under $250
> **$$** $250–$450
> **$$$** over $450

Beacon Hill

The Liberty
M2 **215 Charles St,**
marriott.com · $$

Few successful vacations
involve a stay in jail,
unless you're checking in
here. A former prison
from 1851 to 1990, this
space has been elegantly
revamped, but still wears
its history on its sleeve;
seasonal fare is served at
the restaurant, CLINK,
celebrity mugshots line
the walls of the bar, Alibi,
and the mezzanine has
features of the original
cells. This is a place you'll
willingly stay.

Beacon Hill Hotel
M3 **25 Charles St**
beaconhillhotel.com · $$

If you're looking for an
escape from the hustle
and bustle of Downtown
without leaving the city
center, this hotel, located
in a 19th-century town-
house, is a great choice.
There are just 14 rooms,
each decorated with
carefully chosen pieces
of art and splashes of
color; the bold ceilings
make quite an impact.

XV Beacon
P3 **15 Beacon St**
xvbeacon.com · $$$

This is luxury at its best.
Marble bathrooms?
Check. In-room gas
fireplaces? Check. A
curated pillow menu?
You heard that right.
When you've finished
swooning over your new
bedroom, more treats
await at the restaurant,
where prime cuts of beef
are served alongside
savory seafood dishes.

Back Bay

Raffles Boston
L5 **40 Trinity Pl**
rafflesboston.com
· $$$

This might be a brand
new building, but Raffles
Boston is all about classic
charm, much like Back
Bay itself. After checking
in at the Writer's Lounge,
you're whisked away (by
a personal butler, no
less) to rooms accented
with dark wood, textured
wallpaper, and vintage-
style minibars. Throw
back a Boston Sling in
the Long Bar once you've
settled in.

The Lenox Hotel
L5 **61 Exeter St**
lenoxhotel.com · $

The Lenox has some
serious eco cred.
Hallways feature filtered
water stations, bath-
rooms are stocked with
locally sourced toiletries,
and the restaurant and
bar use honey harvested
from the rooftop bee-
hives. It's a lovely place
to retreat to after seeing
Boston by bike (which
you can rent from the
hotel, by the way).

The Newbury Boston
M4 **1 Newbury St**
thenewburyboston.com
· $$$

One of Boston's hottest
addresses was once
home to the country's
first Ritz-Carlton. Now
owned by the Newbury,
glamor is still at the fore;
designs feature antique
chandeliers and marble
floors, and neighboring
stores include Chanel
and Cartier. The icing on
the opulent cake? The
rooftop restaurant
Contessa, serving up
incredible skyline views.

Mandarin Oriental, Boston

K5 · **776 Boylston St** · **mandarinoriental.com** · **$$$**

Boston is home to its fair share of lavish spas, but there's a reason why the Mandarin Oriental is Massachusetts's first to be awarded five stars by Forbes. Home to a crystal steam room, vitality pools, and 11 treatment rooms, it's the best place to relax after a long day of sightseeing.

North End and the Waterfront

Boston Yacht Haven

R2 · **87 Commercial Wharf** · **thebostonyacht haven.com** · **$$**

Serving as a testament to Boston's rich legacy of seafaring, the Boston Yacht Haven comes complete with a huge marina located steps away from the heart of the North End. While boat owners can moor here overnight, those who prefer to lodge on dry land can enjoy the 10-room inn; some rooms overlook the harbor.

Boston Harbor Hotel

R3 · **70 Rowes Wharf** · **bhh.com** · **$$$**

Hoping to spot a celeb or two during your trip? Look no further than this palatial property, which has become a hot spot for the rich and famous thanks to its world-class seafood restaurant and chandelier-clad Presidential Suite. As a bonus for cartography fans, there's a wall full of antique maps, showcasing Boston's transformation over the years.

Battery Wharf Hotel Boston Waterfront

R1 · **3 Battery Wharf** · **batterywharfhotel-boston.com** · **$**

The North End's tangled 17th-century streets don't have much room for hotels, but the Battery Wharf stands as a notable exception. Its great location offers easy access to the area's top sights, but you'll be in no rush to explore once you're tucking into seafood at the watefront Battery Wharf Grille.

Downtown and the Financial District

Omni Parker House

P3 · **60 School St** · **omnihotels.com** · **$$**

While best known for its seafood, Boston also makes a great dessert, and the Omni Parker House is proof of this. This 1850s-era inn saw the invention of the Boston cream pie (p66), a beloved pastry that later became the state dessert of Massachusetts. But the pie isn't all that delights guests – the hotel is also known for its white marble interior and antique furniture.

The Langham, Boston

Q3 · **250 Franklin St** · **langhamhotels.com** · **$$$**

Luxury comes at a price at the Langham – apt, since this used to be a bank. Carpets inspired by the leaf motif on dollar bills and banker's box drawers lining one of the walls are a nod to the building's past. But, for the most part, the space has been superbly upgraded with marble bathrooms and New England-inspired decor.

The Ritz-Carlton, Boston

P4 · **10 Avery St, Boston** · **ritzcarlton.com** · **$$$**

Tasty cocktails, stunning suites, and a roaring lobby fireplace are all awaiting guests at this lavish property, just steps away from Boston Common. For an extra-special stay, book into a Park View Suite, a huge space that offers fine views of the nation's oldest public park.

The Godfrey Hotel Boston

P4 · **505 Washington St** · **godfreyhotelboston. com** · **$**

The Godfrey blends the old and new seamlessly. To create this hotel, two buildings built in the early 1900s have been united, the interiors spruced up with modern touches like funky art and rooms that you enter using your phone.

Chinatown, the Theater District, and South End

Revere Hotel Boston Common

📍 N5 🏠 2200 Stuart St
🆆 reverehotel.com · $$

Adorned with a massive metallic statue of one of the nation's most memorable Founding Fathers, the Revere Hotel wows visitors with its steampunk-inspired decorations and stunning skyline-facing suites – and the dazzling views aren't just to be admired from the guest rooms. In the warmer months head up to the Rooftop @ Revere, a top drinking and dining spot.

Moxy Boston Downtown

📍 N5 🏠 240 Tremont St
🆆 marriott.com · $

The Moxy's complimentary arrival cocktails, photo booth, and colorful decorations make it a top vacation base for the fun-loving, and its prime location is perfect for the entertainment to continue beyond the hotel walls. Just outside the lobby, catch a show at the iconic Wang Theatre or sip drinks and dance the night away at nearby bars and clubs.

W Boston

📍 N5 🏠 100 Stuart St
🆆 marriott.com · $

This hotel comes with all of the typical W brand flourishes – evening live music, spacious suites, a vibrant cocktail lounge.

But this outpost doesn't let you forget you're in Boston. Rooms are decorated to honor figures from Massachusetts' history, like bed throws inspired by the Boston-formed band Aerosmith, and an on-site beer garden reflects Boston's reputation as a top-notch craft beer city.

The Revolution Hotel

📍 M6 🏠 40 Berkeley St, 02116 🆆 therevolution hotel.com · $

While the South End tends to be on the pricier side, the Revolution Hotel offers cozy – and ultra-colorful – accommodations without draining your bank account. For dinner, either make use of your room's complimentary cookware to craft a homemade meal or head to the hotel restaurant Cósmica for a night of Cal-Mex and margs.

Kenmore and the Fenway

The Verb Hotel

📍 D5 🏠 1271 Boylston St
🆆 theverbhotel.com · $

Rock'n'roll might be alive and well at this music hotel, but these aren't rooms you'll want to trash – every piece of memorabilia here riffs off the Fenway's musical legacy. Guitars, jukeboxes, and concert posters make up the decor, and each room comes with a record player, so you can trawl the hotel's record library to find something to play. If a regular room isn't for you, get escorted "backstage" to your very own trailer, much like a rock legend on tour.

Hotel Commonwealth

📍 D5 🏠 500 Commonwealth Ave 🆆 hotel commonwealth.com · $$$

Calling all sports fans! Hotel Commonwealth serves as the sole official hotel of the Boston Red Sox, drawing players in droves and providing guests with an opportunity to spot some of baseball's most lauded stars. There are three great seafood restaurants here, too, so you may well find yourself dining in the company of the players.

Cambridge and Somerville

The Kendall Hotel

📍 E3 🏠 350 Main St
🆆 kendallhotel.com · $

Always wanted to stay in a firehouse? The Kendall Hotel is the next best thing, housed in the former Engine 7 Firehouse, where 11 of the rooms were once firefighter dormitories. If you're not staying in one of these, there's still plenty of fun regalia throughout, like model trucks and statues of dalmatians (they used to run beside the horse-drawn firefighter carriages to keep the horses calm). Ornate prints and paintings from treasured New England artists round out the cozy Victorian interiors.

Le Méridien Boston Cambridge

📍 D3 🏠 20 Sidney St
🌐 marriott.com · $

For a perfectly located hotel, look no further than Le Méridien. Not only is MIT's storied campus on the doorstep, but a quick stroll takes you to Central Square, where fabulous shops, restaurants, and music venues keep you busy day through night. Be sure to stay in one of those nights, though: the hotel's Amuse restaurant dishes out stunning chicken provençal and mussels Etienne.

The Row Hotel at Assembly Row

🏠 360 Foley St, Somerville
🌐 therowhotelatassembly row.com · $

Somerville's Assembly Row district is known for its high-end restaurants and bars, and the Row Hotel's The Row Bar at Reflections is up there with the best of these. Settle in on a plush seat, order a creative cocktail, and enjoy traditional locally sourced food. It's only open for dinner, so pass the time with a dip in the indoor pool.

The Charles Hotel

📍 B2 🏠 1 Bennett St
🌐 charleshotel.com · $$

Art lovers, this one's for you. The Charles Hotel has wholeheartedly embraced Cambridge's affinity for the finer things in life, with original paintings, drawings, photographs, and even quilts exclusively created for the hotel. Take the self-guided tour of the hotel's art collection to uncover the established artists behind each piece.

Kimpton Marlowe Hotel

📍 F2 🏠 25 Edwin H. Land Blvd 🌐 hotelmarlowe.com · $$

Hoping to keep up your exercise routine while on vacation? Take advantage of Kimpton Marlowe's complimentary bicycles and paddleboards and you'll be pedaling along Cambridge's leafy streets and paddling on the Charles River in no time. When you've tired yourself out, unwind at one of the hotel's wine receptions or movie nights.

South of Boston

The Envoy Hotel

📍 H4 🏠 70 Sleeper St
🌐 theenvoyhotel.com · $$

Few venues offer as gorgeous a setting as the Envoy Hotel, located on Boston's harbor. You'll get spectacular skyline views from the hotel, but the real highlight is ending the day at the Lookout Rooftop, watching the waterfront light up from the comfort of a heated igloo. The hotel interiors are pretty dreamy, too, with a Scandi hygge vibe.

Cambria Hotel Boston

📍 H6 🏠 6 W Broadway
🌐 cambriaboston.com · $

Located steps away from the Broadway "T" station and within easy walking distance of both Fort Point and Southie's main thoroughfare, the Cambria's location makes exploring the city easier than ever. To sweeten the deal, rooftop venue Six West is an ideal sunset-watching spot at day's end.

Omni Boston Hotel at the Seaport

🏠 450 Summer St
🌐 omnihotels.com · $

Food glorious food! Home to six dining venues, the Omni will keep you well fueled for whatever your plans are while in Boston. Think French pastries for breakfast, classic pub fare for lunch, and Mediterranean-American cuisine for dinner.

YOTEL Boston

📍 H4 🏠 65 Seaport Blvd
🌐 yotel.com · $

Cool and lively with guests to match, this affordable spot sums up everything that's great about the Seaport District. The highlight is the lively rooftop bar, Deck 12, which offers live music, weekend brunch, and housemade frosé (a refreshing blend of ice, fruit, and rosé) on Fridays. Cheers to that.

INDEX

Page numbers in **bold** refer to main entries.

ACKNOWLEDGMENTS

This edition updated by

Contributor Jared Ranahan

Senior Editor Alison McGill

Senior Designers Laura O'Brien, Stuti Tiwari

Editors Rachel Laidler, Zoë Rutland, Aimee White

Proofreader Kathryn Glendenning

Indexer Helen Peters

Picture Researcher Manager Taiyaba Khatoon

Senior Picture Researcher Nishwan Rasool

Assistant Picture Research Administrator Manpreet Kaur

Publishing Assistant Simona Velikova

Jacket Designer Laura O'Brien

Jacket Picture Researcher Kate Hockenhull

Senior Cartographer James MacDonald

Cartography Manager Suresh Kumar

Senior DTP Designer Tanveer Zaidi

DTP Designer Vijay Khandwal

Pre-production Manager Balwant Singh

Image Retouching-Production Manager Pankaj Sharma

Senior Production Controller Samantha Cross

Managing Editors Shikha Kulkarni, Beverly Smart, Hollie Teague

Managing Art Editors Gemma Doyle

Senior Managing Art Editor Priyanka Thakur

Art Director Maxine Pedliham

Publishing Director Georgina Dee

DK would like to thank the following for their contribution to the previous editions: Demetrio Carrasco, John Coletti, Paul Franklin, Patricia Harris, David Lyon, Nancy Mikula, Rough Guides/Angus Osborn, Susannah Sayler, Jonathan Schultz, Tony Souter, Linda Whitwam.

The publisher would like to thank the following for their kind permission to reproduce their photographs:

Key: a-above; b-below/bottom; c-centre; f-far; l-left; r-right; t-top

Globe / Blake Nissen 62b, Boston Globe / Craig F. Walker 91tr, Boston Globe / David L. Ryan 88tl, Boston Red Sox / Billie Weiss 12cr, John Coletti 106–107b, Richard T Gagnon 60tl, Paul Marotta 13cla, Massachusetts Conference For Women / Marla Aufmuth 51bl, MediaNews Group / Boston Herald via Getty Images 96tl, 101bl, MediaNews Group / Nancy Lane / Boston Herald 67bl, Moment / J.Castro 67tr, John Powell 122b, Scott Eisen / Stringer 94bl, Stone / Greg Pease 80b, Stringer / Cindy Ord 63br, Sygma / Brooks Kraft LLC 51tr, The Boston Globe / Suzanne Kreiter 57tl.

Getty Images / iStock: APCortizasJr 74tl, Arpad Benedek 40–41t, DenisTangneyJr 133br, E+ / yxyeng 77tl, Christopher Marino 19, Lilia Moscalu 76b, Albert Pego 14bl, Sean Pavone 5, 85t, Marcio Silva 17br, Torresigner 69t.

Gibson House Museum: John Woolf 35bl.

Isabella Stewart Gardner Museum: Sean Dungan 43tl, Sienna Scarff 42.

Legal Sea Foods: Gustav Hoiland 109br.

LesbianNightLife.com/Dorchester Brewing Co: 65tl.

Patricia Harris and David Lyon: 75tr, 94tr, 114tl, 128tl.

New England Aquarium: 46bl.

Pammys: Natasha Moustache 131br.

Photograph © 2024 Museum of Fine Arts, Boston: 37t, 38tl, 38br, 39br.

Shutterstock.com: GCC Photography 133tl, LnP images 87tl, Instagram-TKLVCHV 134t, Lua Carlos Martins 13bl, NoyanYalcin 111br, Panparinda 16ca, Marcio Jose Bastos Silva 23bl, Patrick Yeagle 66tl.

Sweet Cheeks Q: 123tr.

Sheet Map Cover Image:
Whitney R. Shaw: Whitney R. Shaw.

Cover Images:
Front and Spine: **Whitney R. Shaw:** Whitney R. Shaw.
Back: **Alamy Stock Photo:** Péter Mocsonoky tl; **Dreamstime.com:** F11photo tr; **Shutterstock. com:** Sean Pavone cl.

All other images © Dorling Kindersley Limited
For further information see: www.dkimages.com

Illustrator: Lee Redmond

A NOTE FROM DK

The rate at which the world is changing is constantly keeping the DK travel team on our toes. While we've worked hard to ensure that this edition of Boston is accurate and up-to-date, we know that opening hours alter, standards shift, prices fluctuate, places close and new ones pop up in their stead. So, if you notice we've got something wrong or left something out, we want to hear about it. Please get in touch at travelguides@dk.com

First edition 2003

Published in Great Britain by
Dorling Kindersley Limited,
DK, One Embassy Gardens, 8 Viaduct
Gardens, London SW11 7BW, UK

The authorised representative in the EEA is
Dorling Kindersley Verlag GmbH. Arnulfstr.
124, 80636 Munich, Germany

Published in the United States by
DK Publishing, 1745 Broadway, 20th Floor,
New York, NY 10019, USA

Copyright © 2003, 2024 Dorling
Kindersley Limited
A Penguin Random House Company

24 25 26 27 10 9 8 7 6 5 4 3 2 1

The publishers cannot accept responsibility for any consequences
arising from the use of this book, nor for any material on third party
websites, and cannot guarantee that any website address in this
book will be a suitable source of travel information.

A CIP catalog record is available
from the British Library.

A catalog record for this book is available
from the Library of Congress.

ISSN: 1479-344X

ISBN: 978-0-2416-7578-6

Printed and bound in China

www.dk.com

This book was made with Forest
Stewardship Council™ certified
paper – one small step in DK's
commitment to a sustainable future.
Learn more at **www.dk.com/uk/
information/sustainability**